Daily Self Discipline and Procrastination

2-in-1 Book

You Are Not Lazy. Avoid Apathetic Thoughts, Beat Laziness, Break The Distraction Cycle and Get Things Done, Even If you're Lazy AF

Daily Self-Discipline: The Secret Road to Success

Do You Postpone Tasks? No More Unfinished Projects. Discover Cutting-Edge Strategies and Own Your Will Power, Even If you're Lazy AF

Table of Contents

INTRODUCTION 7

CHAPTER 1 – DITCH BAD HABITS NOW 12

    6 Surefire Ways to Quit Bad Habits 12

    3 Essential Steps for Defeating Laziness 18

    How to Stop Procrastinating Now 20

    The 5 Rules of Self-Discipline 23

CHAPTER 2 – DEVELOP A SELF-DISCIPLINE MINDSET 26

    3 Habits That Build Self-Discipline 26

    4 Essential Practices to Ignite Strong Willpower 29

    3 Techniques to Strengthen Your Self-Control 34

    5 Psychological Tricks to Boost Self-Discipline 38

CHAPTER 3 – THE SECRETS OF GOAL-SETTING 44

    How to Create SMART Goals for Better Output 45

    How to Create HARD Goals for Higher Excellence 49

    The Secrets to Turning Your Goals into Achievable Steps 54

    How to Reward Yourself for Progress 57

    4 Ways to Create a Goal-Friendly Environment 61

CHAPTER 4 - TECHNIQUES TO AMP UP OUTPUT 65

Transform Your Life with the Getting Things Done (GTD) Method .. 65

Achieve More with the Pomodoro Technique 70

4 Productive Habits of the Zen-to-Done Method................................. 74

Using the "Don't Break the Chain" Technique for Consistency 78

4 Science-Backed Hacks for Increased Productivity 80

CHAPTER 5 - PLANNING FOR DAILY SUCCESS............................ 84

6 Morning Routines to Start the Day on Top.. 84

4 Evening Routines to End the Day Just Right.................................... 89

Eat These 3 Foods for a Productive Brain 95

15 Daily Affirmations to Teach Your Brain Self-Discipline................ 99

CHAPTER 6 - TOOLS FOR FUTURE SUCCESS.............................. 103

5 Exercises to Test and Maintain Powerful Self-Discipline 103

How to Create Lasting Self-Awareness.. 106

3 Healthy Habits for Better Concentration 110

3 Unconventional Ways to Master Self-Discipline............................. 113

3 Transformative Ways to Push Yourself to the Next Level 116

CONCLUSION.. 119

Introduction

Have you delayed your "big" project only to delude yourself you'll do it when you're ready — and that moment never comes? Have you fallen into a loop of laziness, and can't get anything done? Maybe you started working on your dream project, only to give up 2 to 3 days later? What if you tried to learn a new language like Spanish — but gave up after the first 2 lessons because the grammar was exhausting? Have you ever dreamed of learning to play the guitar, but once you actually sat through the lessons, the chords were too hard to learn and you dropped it halfway? We've all been there!

The secret to sticking to tasks you don't want to do is self-discipline. Everyone will tell you to develop self-discipline; but how do you actually develop atomic-level self-discipline that allows you to overcome each temptation in your daily life? The kind of self-discipline that allows you to create million-dollar projects, stick through daily tasks, and get s%*t done? The secret of atomic self-discipline is revealed in this book. You're in for a journey.

This book teaches you how to handle the hardest part of human nature: Biological impulses. Biological impulses work against you. All humans delude themselves that their thoughts are their own. However,, have you considered that your thoughts are not really your own? Look at what you do instead of what you think in your head: Have you ever thought that you should get fit and should be eating broccoli instead of pizza, but found yourself ordering pizza at midnight? This is not your fault, but the fault of your biological programming. Your biology is wired to respond to immediate pleasure: food, sex, sleep, entertainment. Biological impulses are powerful, and they cannot be overcome easily. Biological impulses run nature; if you observe nature at its purest form, all animals are essentially trying to consume energy or reproduce. The same biological impulses driving us and making life great can also destroy us. This is why self-discipline is key to overcoming our biological programming.

The 5 Grand Revelations of Self-Discipline

Revelation #1: You are your own worst enemy. There are no external forces controlling you, and no one stood in your way. You created all the obstacles yourself. Accept that all your procrastination, inadequacy, failed projects and unmet deadlines are a result of your own lack of self-discipline.

The first step to obtaining self-discipline is to accept you are in a struggle with yourself. Self-discipline is the art of overcoming your own biological impulses. Once a person gets through their main obstacle — biological impulses — they can beat all procrastination, lack of focus, and laziness.

Revelation #2: Human Evolution works against you. Millions of years of evolution have wired our bodies and brains to act in animalistic ways — your nature does not work in your best interest. Essentially, we're wired to take in the most value in exchange for the least amount of effort. To reverse our biological programming, we have to train our brain on reversing the process: We have to maximize output and minimize the value we seek in return.

Once a person's brain is re-wired to exert output rather than seeking the next thing to consume, their productivity goes up and this helps them achieve all their goals. The human body is not just a reflection of two parents having a child, it's also a continuation of millions of years of evolution which you have to struggle to undo. The brain is like a horse: If you let it steer on its own, it will lead you to the edge of a cliff. If you steer it right, it will lead you to your destination. This is why self-discipline is the key to overcoming our evolution and learning to use it to our advantage.

Revelation #3: It never gets easy. Self-discipline is a daily struggle, even after years of training yourself and rewiring your brain, you're going to struggle with discipline daily. This is because you can't detach from millions of years of evolution. Your body was wired to operate a certain way; you can only accept that you're in this for the long term. Reversing evolution is easier said than done, and it's a daily struggle. Even after years of self-discipline and exercise, people will still have a daily fight with themselves. But the main difference is that the fight becomes a lot easier.

Pro Tip: Results are produced in daily increments. Movies have conditioned us to expect a big motivational moment to hit us and, all of a sudden, we're supermen. But in reality, tasks get done with focus and momentum. Once a person rewires their brain to push through daily tasks, their work becomes a breeze.

Revelation #4: Self-discipline builds momentum. People go through loops of high motivation and high downtime/resistance to work. Both of those create momentum. If a person is trying to lose weight by jogging, the first few days might be hard, but once they've gone through the first 2 to 3 days, they build up momentum and it's a lot easier for them to run.

The same applies to work — once a person "warms up" at work by having a very productive day, they can repeat that behavior tomorrow. To be successful, you have to ride the waves of momentum. And once you start you have to create the moment. Each action creates momentum: If you're lazy, you will get momentum of laziness and never do anything. On the other hand, if you are productive, you create more productive momentum. This reflects on a much larger scale. For example, countries that get rich tend to get richer while developing countries tend stay in a loop of poverty.

Revelation #5: Your brain can be rewired for self-discipline. Each action "wires" your brain to accept that as a new habit — and this applies to bad habits and good habits. If a person starts smoking, their immune system will reject the nicotine temporarily. But after a while, the brain will wire-up to accept it and start craving the substance. This creates addiction in the person's brain because their brain is rewired to that of a smoker, even if they've never smoked a cigarette before in their lives.

The brain can also be rewired for good habits. Once the brain is forced to accept a new habit, it finds a million ways to accept it. Has your boss ever threatened that you'd be fired if you fail to complete a task on time? Under pressure, your brain can find a million ways to complete a task. Once you're forced to do something, your brain starts rewiring and allowing you to do the tasks you want. The brain can be rewired to get projects done on time, to focus on hard tasks, avert temptation, and perform at peak levels. This book will teach you to rewire your brain.

How to get Motivation to Start now?

Are you still holding off your life project? Do you feel you're not ready and do you want to start next year or five years from now? Starting now is the key to making it, like the Nike commercial "Just do it."

Life Hack: The key to overcoming all procrastination is a simple mind-shift: *"You're there when you do it."* Remember that phrase.

Daily Self-Discipline

There is no magical time in the future when you'll be "ready" to start a business, to have children, to stop procrastinating, to buy a house, to own Bitcoin, to do the hard tasks. However, once you actually do these simple things, you're immediately at the finish line! When you sell your first product, you're in business. When you go out and jog, you're successful in fitness.

The premise is that you don't have to lie to yourself by setting up an arbitrary future starting point when you can shift the date to right now. The only thing holding you back is your own permission. Give yourself permission to start now and you're already at the finish line. Achieving your goals is as simple as realizing you make it once you take the action, not when the time comes! Will you take action or wait?

Chapter 1 – Ditch Bad Habits Now

Are you struggling with smoking, pulling your hair, eating badly, or oversleeping? If your problems are simple and come down to one bad habit, you can solve it by rooting out that bad habit.

Habits are actions we do repetitively. Once a person repeats a certain action multiple times, it becomes a habit. Once a person repeats a habit for longer periods such as months or years, it becomes their identity. Many times, people can't remember what their life was like before they assumed their bad habits as part of their identity.

Habits can be good or bad. A good habit is to wake up early in the morning, or work hard at your job, to eat moderately, to meditate. A bad habit is to wake up late, consume substances you don't need, harm yourself, or engage in activities that deplete your quality of life.

To be effective in eliminating bad habits, we have to pull bad habits like weeds by grabbing the root and removing them from the ground up. We don't want to pull at the top of the weed, giving it an opportunity to regrow. All habits can be completely rooted out by changing your identity and rewarding yourself with each milestone. This chapter focuses on the shift in identity a person should make in order to quit bad habits.

6 Surefire Ways to Quit Bad Habits

1) Create a New Identity

To root out a bad habit, you have to do one important thing — create a new identity for yourself. If you don't create a new identity and you stick to your old identity, you'll be prone to relapsing and repeating the same mistakes. Smokers who want to quit almost never create a non-smoker identity; they imagine themselves as smokers who "gave up" smoking. They've smoked for years and associate every moment in life with smoking: coffee breaks, work breaks, friend gatherings, parties, travel, etc.

However, they have to tap into the part of their brain that remembers what it used to be like as a non-smoker; they need to go back to when they were younger as most people start smoking in their teens. Could you remember the time you didn't need a cigarette in the morning when you were only happy with a cup of coffee and you weren't tempted when you saw others smoking? That was way back when you didn't assume a smoker's identity. Now that you took the identity of a smoker, you find it hard to quit.

Bad habits are essentially rooted out by reversing the clock and going back to the time when you didn't do them. If you don't remember, then you need to create a new identity that separates you from your old identity that repeated these mistakes.

Bad habits destroy lives: Alcohol, gambling, smoking, drugs, bad food. People know what they're doing is not good for them, but that information is useless — the habit is too strong and they fall back in the same behavioral patterns. In order to not fall in repetitive behavior, they have to step back and create an ANTI-IDENTITY to their current identity. Anti-identity is a method to take your current identity and live by the opposite principles. If you're a smoker, take on the identity of a NON-SMOKER. If you're a gambler, take on the identity of an ANTI-GAMBLER. If you're an alcoholic, take on the identity of a SOBER person.

Pro Tip: You don't have to "hate" your previous habit. Many people create negative energy and hate against their previous habits to cope with their new identity. However, if you really assume your new anti-identity, you can "detach" from your previous habit completely and without emotional baggage. Even years after you quit your bad habit, you might still be tempted. But the difference is that you'll be tempted at the same level as a person who was never addicted to a bad habit. This means that you will be underwhelmed in your temptation.

2) Plan Future Actions

To create a new identity, you have to have a positive outlook on your future that will allow you to take the action necessary to quit bad habits. If you have a positive mindset, you are more likely to be successful. How do you get a positive mindset? Think of the positive benefits that will come from you ditching your bad habit. Think about what your daily life will look like.

Pro Tip: Think about what your daily life will look like and write your ideal day down on a piece of paper. Write down where you'd wake up, what you would do in the morning, how you would live. Create a visual image in your head for what your new life is supposed to look like.

There are benefits to visualizing your new identity: If you're a smoker, you will get many benefits from your future non-smoker identity. You'll breathe easier, you'll become healthier, your breath won't smell, you won't spend money on cigarettes, you won't be at the mercy of nicotine addiction, etc. The bad habits probably create more negatives in your life than positives; if you want you can make a chart and compare the positives of your bad habit (the emotional value it gives you) with the negatives. If the negatives outweigh the positives, ditch the habit.

3) Push Through Resistance

This is the hardest part of quitting a habit — the initial resistance. When you stop a bad habit such as substance addiction, your body will go into "withdrawal" and have you craving for the substance. This is when you're most vulnerable to relapse. People who quit for a while can maybe last a full week; but after four weeks or more, they might relapse because they're constantly tempted by external forces. For example, a smoker might see their friends smoking or a commercial of people enjoying cigarettes. They have to fight the resistance, which is the strongest the first month.

Once a person has dropped a habit for over a month, they can start to assume a new identity. The first month is the real test to your resistance and the temptation will be at its strongest. Expect it. If a person can go through a full month without a bad habit, they will likely create a new identity and sustain it for the rest of their lives. You must push through resistance, and remember that the negatives of your habit far outweigh the positives; this should be enough to keep you from repeating bad habits.

4) Replace Bad Habits

If you push through resistance, you're not done! You still have to replace a habit.

Pro Tip: People think its "willpower" that creates good habits, but good habits are created by replacing bad habits with new habits. Instead of giving your body your addiction, give it something else it doesn't crave. This will stimulate it the same, but the effect on your body won't be negative.

The best way to replace a bad habit is to create a replacement habit that will be good for the body. Many addictions are hard to shake off because they provide a high level of stimulus for the nerves and brain that make it impossible to quit. To replace those habits, you have to hit your body with equal stimulus but positive.

For example, many people who quit smoking say they did it with cold showers. Don't believe it? Cold showers that last three to five minutes in freezing cold can severely affect the nervous system to such a degree that the person feels literally no need for nicotine at all — the body has had its dose of stimulation.

Many drug addicts quit only by exercising or cold showering. This is easier said than done because a cold shower takes getting used to. You first have to smear water on your body by hand so you don't dive straight in the cold. Once you're used to it, you can go for small increments of cold. The cold will make you shiver, and it will shake up your entire nervous system. This helps with all substance addictions like nicotine, alcohol, even heroin.

Smaller bad habits like nail-biting and hair-twisting can be replaced by getting a squeezable ball that you scratch or play with instead. This will keep your hands away from your mouth and hair, and allow you to get your stimulation without harming your body.

5) Reward Yourself

Rewarding yourself is not a feel-good tactic; this is not something you do to celebrate but to re-wire your brain that the actions you're taking are good. If you're suffering all the time, if your addiction is eating you alive from the withdrawal, you must reward yourself incrementally in order to not burn out. Rewarding yourself is for the finish line: Once you've lasted a few days or a few weeks without a bad habit, it's time to give yourself a treat. You should endure suffering, and end it by treating yourself to something good.

Pro Tip: Treat yourself to a vacation if you gave up a bad habit. Book a flight to a new city or the beach, and spend a few days reminiscing at how good of a job you did. This will re-assert your new identity and keep you from slipping back into old habits.

If you suffer endlessly and you never reward yourself, you will burn out. You have to treat your brain like an animal; the horse only carries people and allows itself to be whipped because it expects a meal at the end of the day. If you promise yourself a treat after you go x amount of days without a bad habit, the reward mechanism will keep you going. This ties into a positive mindset.

6) Create a Milestone Action Plan

A long-term milestone plan is about sustaining your new identity. If you create new habits to replace your bad habits, you must keep them until the new-found identity is irreversible and part of your core being.

Planning for the long-term will allow you to create a new identity and sustain it. Think about your replacement habit: If you started with cold showers to quit an addiction, allocate a certain time of the night to repeat the cold showers. For example, your long-term strategy could be to shower at 10 PM every night: This is all you need in order to sustain your habit. The minute you make excuses or step off the habit, you will be prone to resistance and relapsing. Long-term resistance planning is all about finding a replacement habit and working on it constantly. If you achieve a 7-day milestone, give yourself a reward for that milestone. To be effective, you must assume you have a new anti-identity that is the opposite of your identity which created bad habits.

3 Essential Steps for Defeating Laziness

Do you have trouble getting out of bed in the morning for work? Do you struggle meeting deadlines of a project? Are you jobless and find it hard finding a job, or do you not feel like going to interviews at all? Laziness is a mental handicap; it can destroy your life because success is built on the opposite — work and productivity.

To stop being lazy, you have to change your mindset. Laziness cannot be treated at the surface level. If you take Adderall to focus or watch motivational videos, you're only going to last the few days or weeks until your supply runs out or you start feeling side-effects. Then your motivation will dip again, and you'll slip back to your old habits again. This is why you need a long-term identity change.

To solve laziness, you have to look at what causes it. This is an uglier side of laziness — you might be lazy because bad things have happened to you in the past. These past events/traumas or existential crisis may have created in you low self-esteem and a nihilistic mindset. Once you discover what your root cause is, you can work on eliminating it. Temporary fixes such as prescription pills will only last for a short time, and let's not even go into the negative aspects of prescription pills and other "focus" pharmaceuticals.

1) Identify the Cause of Laziness

To identify the root of your laziness; think about the history of when you started your bad habits — Did you get in a rut after you got fired from a job or you suffered from a break-up in a relationship? Did you move into a new city/country and had a hard time adjusting to the environment? How long have you been "sinking" in your bad habits? Think about the time before that, and what you used to be like. This will create a clear image for where you need to revert to. Simply take a week off to consider this, take a small trip out in nature and meditate on your behavior. You will realize where it went downhill and correct your bad habits. If you were always lazy, you will have to do the opposite — create a new identity to break the laziness.

Pro Tip: For most people, laziness is caused by a lack of mental clarity. Focus can be influenced by nutrition; food has a direct impact on the functioning of the brain. Bad food makes the brain unclear and this is why successful people overspend on good expensive foods.

2) Maximize Time in a Day

This is the most important step — not wasting time. Without realizing it, you're wasting five or maybe 10 hours of each day doing things that benefit you in no significant way. Worst of all, you might spend 10 hours a day doing nothing. How many times have you refreshed your Instagram feed today? How many times have you swiped on Tinder or talked to your colleagues when you should've been working? You might not realize this, but you've probably wasted a dozen hours you could've used productively.

To maximize time in a day, you have to shift your mindset from that of a consumer to that of a producer. A "consumer" mindset is about consuming external influences: social media, entertainment, movies, food, news, etc. A "producer" mindset is about output flowing out of you: making products, selling products, inventing, designing, creating, writing, editing. The producer mindset enables you to be at the root of life: You create the entertainment people are consuming, you create the social media content, you create the products they use, and you create the trends they follow. When you create value, people want to give you value in return. This is a key mind shift you have to make to be successful. Once you switch into a producer mindset, you'll appreciate your time a lot more.

3) Plan Productive Days

The way to do this is to act proactively. Your nutrition and bad habits could have a very negative effect on your focus and brain. High carbohydrate foods such as pasta, bread, pastries, and sugary drinks make your brain "clouded" and fuzzy. With these foods, it's almost impossible to focus. Your struggles might have come from the consumption of those foods. The worst part is that they're so widespread that the average person isn't even aware of how food can affect mental clarity. Meanwhile, foods such as broccoli, spinach, and steak reinforce your focus and simultaneously boost your mental clarity.

Once you've cleared your mind with good nutrition, you can plan out your daily routine. Start by waking up early and fixing your evening schedule. If you go to bed at midnight, you'll find it very hard to wake up at 6 AM. However, if you go to bed at 10 to 11 PM you'll find it a lot easier to wake up at 6 AM. You can plan your productive days by planning the nutrition you'll consume on those days, the time you'll wake up, the time you'll do your tasks and your work breaks. Once you've planned your days, it all comes down to execution.

How to Stop Procrastinating Now

Have you wasted years procrastinating on your "big" project? How about your job — do you delay work to the last second until the deadline is up, and then you rush it in an all-nighter? Do you have an idea for an invention but can't get yourself to start even after years of thinking about it? Procrastination is a disease that takes root in your brain and spreads like a cancer. Once it spreads to one cell, it spreads to your entire body and kills you. To eliminate the disease, you have to kill it at the start by not letting it take root.

1) Start Immediately

To stop procrastinating, you have to get in the flow immediately. Once your brain accepts that you've started working, it's going to find ways to keep you working. If you delay your project until the afternoon or evening, you'll probably delay it for the next day. This creates a never-ending loop of procrastination and you could waste entire months or years in this loop. Do you know of people who talk about one "business idea" or another but never do anything? They've been infected with the disease of procrastination.

All you have to do to stop procrastinating is to rewind the clock from a future "start point" to a current "start point." Do it right now! Drop everything you're doing — shut off your TV, tell your friends you're not going out, lock yourself in a room and START NOW. Don't delay this until the next day or the next week. Remember the phrase: "There is no better time to start than the present moment." You're prepared already and you must take action. Once you've started, you've done 90% of the work. The rest is all about building your momentum.

2) Optimize Your Time

The way you spend your time is unpredictable. You might think that you'll wake up in the morning and be productive, but turns out you only end up drinking coffee and watching YouTube videos until the afternoon. This is why you have to allocate key actions to exact time frames to optimize your time. If you take out a piece of paper and break down your day by the hour, you would be a lot more productive.

For example, you wake up at 6 AM, drink coffee, start work at 7 AM, work for 2 hours, take a 30-minute break at 9 AM, and continue working until 12 NN. Write this down on paper. Optimizing your time makes it impossible to fail because you'll devise a plan for every hour of the day. If you only tell yourself you'll get it done in the morning; you'll probably make up an excuse or do something else. Once your day is written in paper, you can actually execute based on that. Tell yourself that even if you don't finish your task in the time frame you allocated but you spent all that time working, that you still did a good job. Reward yourself every time you execute on your schedule.

3) Split Your Projects into Small Pieces

If you try to do everything at once, the projects will overwhelm you unless you split them in small pieces, which may mean spending a whole day working on a tiny part of a project. For example, if you have to write a 15-page business plan, start by writing 5 pages the first day, then write 5 pages the next day, and 5 pages the day after. In 3 days, you'll be done! This is much more realistic than forcing the whole project in 1 day.

If you load yourself on too much work, you'll find it harder to focus, and you'll lose motivation because you'll think you're not making progress. However, when you split your project into multiple pieces, you can check them off like a checklist. Reward yourself every time you complete a piece of a project by taking a break, or going for a walk. Eventually, you'll tackle entire projects by learning how to allocate them in smaller bits.

The 5 Rules of Self-Discipline

Self-discipline is about beating resistance, taking control of your emotions and doing what's right for the greater good. Self-discipline is not only practiced by Buddhists, martial artists, or athletes — it's also for the average person who wants to be successful. Self-discipline is an art form, and once a person understands what it consists of, they can start implementing it in their daily lives.

1) Self-Discipline Is a Sacrifice

To discipline yourself you have to sacrifice all your comforts and pleasures. You'll no longer be able to oversleep, overeat or indulge in negative habits. You have to sacrifice everything you knew as your "comfortable life." Self-discipline is not a getaway that you do for 1 week and then revert back to your life of comfort; it's a life-long task and the art of reshaping your identity.

To develop self-discipline, you'll have to go through literal hell and you'll encounter resistance on each step. Voices in your head will tempt you to go back to your bad habits — to procrastinate and not do what's right — but if you sacrifice long enough, you will learn to ignore them. This is why self-discipline essentially boils down to sacrifice.

2) Self-Discipline Is an Identity Change

Self-discipline is not about making your current life work. People think that there are "tricks" and "shortcuts" to keep their existing way of living without making radical changes on their identity and way of operating. If you're not prepared to fully change your life by changing your sleep schedule, nutrition habits, work habits and thought patterns, the chance you'll succeed with self-discipline is very little. Self-discipline is about changing your entire modus operandi, not making your current one work.

3) If You Know Why, You'll Know How

If you want self-discipline, ask yourself: Why do you want self-discipline? Is it to become a better person? Is it to do better at your job? Is it to quit a bad habit that impacts your health? Ask yourself: Why are you trying to achieve this? If you don't know the answer, you'll only be spinning your wheels like a hamster trapped in a cage and not getting anywhere. Once you know what you're trying to achieve, your brain will know that the sacrifice is worth it. Keep your end goal in mind every time you're tempted to sip back into your old habits.

4) Self-Discipline Has to Be Realistic

Be careful not to overwhelm yourself with unrealistic goals. If you work hard daily and expect to become a millionaire in one year, you might find that it's not going to happen. If you try to quit smoking and you quit cold turkey, you might want to start by smoking less the first few weeks and then letting go completely. In order to get the motivation to stick at a new habit, your brain requires proof that you can survive the change. Your brain doesn't care that you "think" you'll do it; it wants to experience the change firsthand. Do this, and your brain will give you the motivation to stick at a new habit. Start by taking small increments and then go radical, instead of ramping up on your changes from the beginning.

5) Doing What You Don't Want Produces Results

If you look back in life at all your hard tasks — the all-nighters you had to stay up to finish a project; the gym sessions that got you 6-pack abs; the hard jobs you did to make money — they probably all came from doing tasks that you didn't want to do. They were probably difficult to do. In essence, the hardest jobs and the things we want to do the least are the ones that produce the most results for us. If you can discipline yourself to focus exclusively on productive tasks and activities that increase your output, you can maximize your life quality and productivity.

Chapter 2 – Develop A Self-Discipline Mindset

Self-discipline is a skill, one that can be learned like riding a bike. Learn self-discipline as if you're trying to learn to ride a bike or swim in the ocean — it takes time to cultivate the skill. If you don't know how to swim, how do you start? You dip in the water and start practicing. Then you stay afloat for a while, and repeat until you can swim. You build the momentum to practice more until you're a swimmer. Self-discipline is based on 2 things: daily practice and momentum. To obtain self-discipline, a person has to hone their skills to build consistency and small-step their way until they've mastered the skill.

Why does a person need self-discipline? The answer: it helps you achieve difficult things like giving up your bad habits or performing better at your job. In order to achieve your goals, discipline is required. Self-discipline can be trained like any other habit; the key to success is perseverance. Once you strengthen your self-discipline, you'll be able to do things in life such as get rid of your bad habits, increase your productivity, and become fit and happy. Self-discipline is hard as it reshapes your mind to go beyond your basic emotional needs.

3 Habits That Build Self-Discipline

Pro Tip: To develop self-discipline, treat your brain as if you're an athlete and you need daily training to compete in the sport championship. What happens when an athlete misses their daily training? They fall out of shape. Give yourself time if you're just starting, and kick yourself in the butt when you're slacking.

The following are the #3 essential skills to develop a self-discipline mindset:

1) The "One Day to Success" Habit

The self-discipline mindset is managed on the macro: You have to prepare your brain for the long-term, but act in small daily increments. The #1 technique to obtain self-discipline what we call the "One day to success" habit:

- **The One Day to Success Habit: "If you did it for one day, treat yourself as if you're already successful."**

If you stick to your diet for one day, be as happy as if you've already lost weight. Don't wait until you have a shiny 6-pack to give yourself a pat on the back. Long-term success is built on small daily success and it makes sense to celebrate once you've gone through a full day of discipline. Measure your success based on what you've done in a day — if you've successfully disciplined yourself, treat yourself as if you already achieved your goal. Did you do your work today? If you completed your tasks, act as if you're already at the finish line.

This is a mind shift that will get your mind to build momentum by acting as if you made it once you've gone through a full day of self-discipline. Large successes are built on daily milestones. The wrong approach is to wait for 30 days or 6 months until you reward yourself and say you've made it. The right approach is to discipline yourself for a day and then pat yourself on the back for your accomplishments that day. Base your self-esteem and happiness on your daily tasks. If you did everything you needed to do for the day, consider yourself successful. If you failed, try again tomorrow.

2) Kill Instant Gratification

Human nature wires us to consume things that provide us immediate gratification: Bad foods, alcohol, cigarettes, the news, movies, social media — what do these all have in common? They provide instant emotional relief and gratification. Self-discipline is the art of optimizing your mind for delayed, long-term gratification. If you eat a candy bar that you know you're not supposed to eat, you'll be gratified instantly. If you say no to the candy and consume broccoli instead, you'll get a better body in 30 days. The difference is that you'll be gratified later. Discipline is different from self-control because in self-control we exercise restraint, while with self-discipline we essentially re-wire our brain for discipline for the long term.

Self-discipline is a life-long task that challenges our mind continually. Accept that as long as you're alive, your mind will always push you to take the way of instant gratification — that's your biology following a survival instinct. We always want to eat because back when we used to live in tribes, if we didn't eat, we'd die. We always want to have sex because if we didn't, we wouldn't reproduce. We are addicted to substances and social media because they ping our brain with dopamine chemicals that signal we're safe. The key is not to change our biology, but to observe it objectively and take control of it.

Pro Tip: Become God. Imagine yourself as God watching your room from above. To beat our biology, we have to observe our impulsive behaviors from a 3rd person perspective: Where are you at right now? You're in a room, you are reading a book. If you go to the kitchen, observe your behavior. Ask yourself: Is this person doing something rational, or are they acting primitive? Take control of your bad behavior by removing your identity from your actions, and looking at yourself through the prism of a neutral entity.

3) Create Momentum Waves

Once you've achieved your daily success, repeat the same process by pushing through your daily milestones. This will create "Momentum Waves" that you ride like a surfer catching a wave in the open ocean. Find a big wave and catch it. If you fall off, climb back on. If you exercise for 1 day, repeat your actions diligently for a week. This will create huge momentum for you to keep going for a full month. Once you've done it for a month, keep going for a full year.

Do you remember when you used to be at peak of your productivity at work, you kept producing on time, you were making money and your clients/boss were praising your work? You were in what's called a "momentum wave." Once you get the initial momentum, it's impossible to stop. Self-discipline creates momentum. If you push a rock down a mountain, the rock will start off slow but then the speed will accelerate. By the time the rock hits the ground it can be going at an upwards of 300 mph.

Once you start with daily self-discipline exercises, you will start slow, but persevere until the momentum builds and it will become natural for you to do the tasks that you previously deemed "hard." Essentially, we're in a battle with your biological wiring and minds on the daily. Once you realize there is no "permanent fix" (i.e. a solution that alleviates you of the daily struggle against your nature), and that this a life-long task, you learn to anticipate the daily challenge and create momentum gradually. Take it one day at a time.

4 Essential Practices to Ignite Strong Willpower

What do you do when you don't feel like doing something? How do you find the energy to go to the gym at night when you feel like sleeping and staying inside? How do you get up at 5 AM to go prepare for work when you want an extra hour of sleep? How do you get the motivation to do those things you're supposed to, and do them consistently? The answer is willpower. Willpower can be the deciding factor between a successful goal and a failed goal.

What is the difference between a millionaire CEO who runs his own company and a homeless person on the street? The difference is willpower. One has the willpower to push through and be successful, while the other one lacks willpower and can barely function in life. Some people want to be successful, and they know what it takes to be successful - but they lack the willpower to do it. This chapter focuses on the importance of willpower and top 4 techniques to develop willpower to push through your daily tasks.

Willpower is like a muscle in the brain. It becomes weak when left untrained. If you do nothing to practice your willpower, you will slack and be unproductive. Treat your brain as a vehicle and willpower as the motor: If you don't have a motor, or if you have a half-functioning motor, you won't be able to drive the vehicle. However, if the motor is well-oiled and the mechanics are functioning - you'll be able to drive your vehicle through the roughest terrain in the mountains. The same applies for your brain - when you have willpower, you have a functioning brain that will get you to do anything. Want to be able to wake up at 5 AM and feel great? Want to be able to exercise at night and look forward to your trip to the gym? Want to be able to work 10 hours without breaks or distractions? Fix your willpower – and you can achieve it.

Pro Tip: Treat willpower like a bicep. To increase muscle mass, you have to lift weights in areas that target the biceps. If you stop lifting weights, your muscles shrink. The same applies to willpower: You must put pressure on your brain to develop the willpower, but once you've developed it, the practice becomes easier. If you stop working on your willpower, you lose it and you fall off. Willpower requires constant discipline and daily sacrifice.

Daily Self-Discipline

Willpower has to be built gradually - one doesn't develop willpower overnight. Be careful not to be too overwhelmed, even if the goals seem realistic. For example, if your goal is to exercise at 9 PM sharp every night, make sure that you don't burn yourself out too much or you might not be able to exercise tomorrow. Take breaks and reward yourself once every few days, in order to not burn out. Start by taking small increments, and build your willpower using the techniques below gradually. Once you gain momentum, continue doing it and the actions will become a part of your identity.

Remember the 6-month rule: What seemed hard for you to do today will become an average day for you in 6 months. If you thought running and lifting weights in one day is impossible, once you get yourself to do it once - you might find this is an average day for you after 6 months; and you'll add another activity on top. Your willpower will peak after your brain has evidence it's possible. To give it evidence, you must throw yourself in the line of fire every day. You will naturally have dips in the process, and you must pick yourself up. Once your momentum dips, force yourself to do it again and your willpower will peak.

1) Give Your Brain Proof, Not Promises

Remember this phrase: "**Your brain wants proof, not promises.**" Your brain works like a coin machine: Once it's given proof that something is possible, it gives willpower in return. If you tell yourself "I will eat better today", your brain won't notice and give you the willpower to do it. However, if you force yourself to do it - you cook healthy food and consume it; your brain will have definite proof that it's possible. Then, it will naturally provide you the willpower to repeat it the next day. Your brain is in constant demand for proof that you can do certain things, and you must feed it physical proof if you want to get the willpower in return. Have you tried quitting smoking? If you actually stopped smoking for 1 week, your brain would have all the proof it needs to give you the willpower to be a non-smoker forever. It's not enough to think positively and make reaffirmations that you'll do it one day. You must take physical action in order for your brain to supply you with the willpower you need.

Force yourself to do what's right for one day, and your willpower will increase dramatically. If you're back from vacation and lacking willpower to go back to work, force yourself to work immediately. You will work one day faced with resistance, but your brain will have proof that it's possible. Then your willpower will return and you'll be able to go back to work the same as you used to. If you haven't exercised in 2 years, and you've fallen out of shape, you can re-set your workout routine by going out at night. Find a jogging path, get dressed and start exercising. Once you've gone through your first night, your willpower to repeat the process will rise exponentially.

2) Start With Uncomfortable Tasks

What happens when you start work in the morning? You feel discomfort. What happens when you start jogging on the track? You feel discomfort. What happens when you go for a job interview? You feel discomfort. Discomfort is what you need; it means the action is worth pursuing. Now think about what happens when you push through discomfort - you become comfortable with the habit and you start engaging with it. The discomfort you're feeling in this case is not caused by lack of ideal circumstance — it's caused by your own biological resistance. Biological resistance tries to chain you in place and conserve energy, so you must do the opposite of what you're feeling inside your body.

Remember this: **Your body does not care about your goals.** Your body rewards you for doing things that actually stall your progress:

Sleeping, eating junk food, smoking, drinking, consuming media. Your biology is wired to get you to release the least amount of energy and consume as much energy as possible. Have you ever wondered why you want to do less at work, why you sleep late, why you want to stay in bed instead of hitting the gym? It's because the resistance is there to prevent you from releasing surplus energy that would actually get you to be successful in life.

Pro Tip: To be successful, do the reverse of what your biology wires you to do. Want to sleep? Get out of bed. Want to eat pizza? Cook broccoli instead. Want to stay inside and not exercise? Go out to the gym. Want to watch Netflix and slack off? Go work 10 hours straight without taking any breaks.

Tune in with your body, listen to what it craves biologically. In most cases you're doing things based on biological impulse, and if you engineer your actions to do the reverse of your impulses, you will create the willpower you need to be successful. Start with uncomfortable tasks, whether it's waking up earlier, doing a hard project at work that you've delayed, or going to the gym. This way the uncomfortable becomes the norm and you never fall prey to your biological impulses.

3) Give 100% Effort in Every Task

Willpower is not only about starting - it's about finishing your tasks at 100% diligence. How do you develop the willpower to do a task, if not by giving your best? The wrong approach is to start an uncomfortable task and slack through, thinking that by delaying the task you can still get it done another day. The right approach is to work as if your life depends on it.

Imagine someone put a gun to your head and told you, "Go out to the gym and do 150 pushups, lift 5 reps and run 10 miles." Would you find the willpower to do it? You definitely would, as your life is under threat. Treat your regular work tasks as if your life depends on your performance, and give your best performance even if the task is unimportant. Once you get used to doing everything at 100% capacity, it leaks into other areas of your life and your willpower to do many things at once skyrockets. You'll develop the willpower to work, exercise, date and engage in fun projects without running out of energy.

4) Cut Off Distractions

Remove all distractions that restrain you from completing your work. Once you've gone through an hour or two of work, you'll feel tempted to take a break and indulge in "relaxation" periods. The downside to this is that it's usually more distractions that arise once you discover one distraction. If you're scrolling on Instagram, you'll find your ex posting something that makes you emotional or an ad that encourages you to travel to Bali. You're suddenly on a booking page searching for flights to Bali - one distraction leads to another until you've completely lost track of your original work. To avoid this, treat everything as if it has a "snowball" effect that can potentially erode your attention and harm your focus just by looking at one thing. Remember how you develop momentum in willpower? The bad side is that you can also develop momentum in distractions, so watch that you're on the right end of that spectrum.

3 Techniques to Strengthen Your Self-Control

Self-control is about controlling your emotional impulses. Look back at your impulsive decisions. Do you eat pizza at 11 PM and wonder why you did it? Do you start smoking at a party and you've been trying to quit? Do you order something on eBay when you know you should be conserving money? This is what's known as impulsive behavior. To obtain self-control over impulsive behavior, you must take control of your emotions. Most emotions that cause impulsive decisions are hard to control as they're driven by anxiety, fear, stress or even happiness. Once you're feeling high on an emotion, it's hard to make rational decisions.

Pro Tip: Self-control is a *preventive* measure. One must observe their behavior to take control of their impulsiveness. Self-control is essential and impervious to making big changes in life, as the daily struggle of self-discipline is tied to making small self-control decisions of restraint. How do you last a full day on a diet, when so many food choices are available? How do focus on work for 10 hours, when you're distracted by social media? How do stop a habit that harms you, when it provides you with good emotions? The answer is simple - overcome your impulsive behavior. There are techniques to overcome your impulsiveness, by observing your behavior and correcting it before it takes over your logical senses.

Self-control is about to averting impulsive behavior. There are 3 steps to avert impulsive behavior:

1) Identify Your Triggers

Impulsive behavior is caused by a lack of logical judgment. When you think rationally, you know what's bad and good for you. Human nature is often more powerful than the rational mind and this is why it's so hard to overcome. The struggle of overcoming nature is tied to our biology, as we've evolved to seek instant gratification. Essentially, most things that feel good are bad for us in the long run. Impulsive behavior can only be corrected on the logical level, by making your rational mind more powerful than your physical urges. How do you achieve this? Start by applying logic. Identify your triggers in advance and act preemptively — avoid putting yourself in a situation where you're tempted.

For example, if you're trying to quit smoking, you might find that partying and getting drunk makes you want to smoke more. Avoid parties — that's your trigger. If you want to eat clean, don't pass by bakeries or other food stores that tempt you to buy food. If you eat at night, get a healthy meal in advance or go to bed early. Identify your little "triggers," the small events that cause your impulsive behavior, and prevent them by completely cutting down on them. Many times, you're exposing yourself to the wrong influences, by consuming media online that serves as launch-ground for bad behavior. Humans are influenced on a subconscious level too; if one sees their friends doing something on social media their brain tempts them to repeat their behavior. Cut of all influences that trigger impulsive behavior.

If the fault of the trigger is on yourself and you can't avoid external stimulus (it's not parties or stores tempting you but your own behavior) the solution is simple: suppress your emotions. Most urges disappear within 10 minutes. If you want to have a smoke, wait it out and occupy yourself with another activity. You only have to observe your desire to smoke, and surpass your emotions. Ideally you should avoid all external triggers and suppress your inner emotions to completely avoid sipping back into impulsive behavior.

2) Restrain Impulsive Behavior

Impulsive behavior is temporary. Taking control of impulsive behavior is essential to self-control as it signifies you dominating over your primal urges. There are two ways to control impulsive behavior: 1) Let it pass 2) Engage in another activity.

Observing your impulsiveness in the 3rd person can give you insight about how you operate and the way to suppress your urges. If you can remove your identity from the equation and look at yourself as if you're neutral person - would you still feel the same urges? Feel the urge as if you're 100% there and present with it, without resisting it. In meditation this practice is known as "becoming present to the moment." This will set your mind at rest because you'll know that your addictions and impulsiveness are nothing more than the result of biological impulses flaring up. The mind attaches personal stories to your impulsiveness, but in essence, it is a behavior driven by the brain's need for fast gratification.

Utilizing replacement activities is an effective way to control impulsive behavior: Go for a shower, take a walk, have a nap, go jogging, buy a boxing bag to punch, talk to someone, etc. There are many ways to regain emotions that you seek from your addiction or impulsiveness in a manner that doesn't harm you.

3) Prevent Future Relapse

Why quit smoking if you're going to relapse after 1 month? Why eat organic food if you're reverting back to junk food a month from now? Relapse is your biggest long-term threat, so knowing how to anticipate relapse is as essential as identifying your triggers. The way you control your behavior will shape your destiny, and anticipating future relapse can help you from sipping back into bad habits.

The way to prevent relapse is simple - change your identity. Many people mistakenly hold on to their old identity and try to "make it work" by changing their habits. However, the only way to succeed in long-term change is to change who you are as a person. You must let go of your current identity and become something else, similar to a caterpillar shaping into a butterfly. For example, if you want to quit smoking you can use techniques to avoid buying cigarettes and going to the store or visiting parties. You can even tell yourself that it's bad for you mentally and that it's a terrible habit. However, the right approach is to assume a non-smokers identity. Do you have friends who don't smoke at all? Do they ever feel tempted by smokes? The answer is no. This is because their identity is fundamentally that of non-smokers. Assume the identity of a person you want to become, and you will lose your current temptations naturally.

5 Psychological Tricks to Boost Self-Discipline

To build on your self-discipline and self-control, psychology can add a layer of willpower that will help you power through the hardest days when you're pushed to the limits of your emotional capacity. What happens when you burst through a week of successful self-discipline, and then you hit a breaking point and relapse on bad habits? The way to avoid that is to apply psychological building blocks — little techniques that when stacked on top of each other, can serve as a foundation for your psychological health. Think of psychological building blocks as bricks. If you had no self-discipline in the past, you can start building your structure by making it for one day. Once you've made it past a day, you can add one more brick. At the end you'll have a whole house.

Remember the phrase: "**The mind is a creature of habit.**" Once your mind is trained to do something, it can also be un-trained. If you've fallen into bad habits, you can reverse the damage by creating entirely new habits. This is because the brain is not definite and can be altered to your ideal form, in order to take back control over your life. Self-discipline is about taking control of the mind, and psychology specializes in studying the mind.

Psychological tricks are not about going to the crazy scientist that lives next door and have them hook you on electrodes that change your mind. Instead, you need to realize that changes can be made gradually. You once didn't drink alcohol — you taught yourself how to do it. You didn't even drink coffee — now, you can't go a day without 2 cups of coffee. The mind is very flexible and can adapt to harmful habits - the same as it can adapt to new "hard" habits which you're trying to enforce that would improve your life. If you have little power over the rational mind, the following psychological tricks can help you take control now:

1) Become Present With Meditation

How do you avoid bad thoughts that lead you to impulsive behavior? The answer is to not have any thoughts at all. Meditation is the art of becoming present and dropping the conscious mind, effectively trusting that your subconscious will be enough to help you make the right decisions. Our minds are preoccupied with thoughts about the future and the past. We spend too much time thinking and little time acting.

Meditation is an exercise that helps us minimize our thoughts, and the exercise of meditation is about focusing on the breath and not thinking for 20 minutes. To visualize presence, imagine yourself in the Caveman days - you were hunting an animal, you had a spear and the animal ran from you. Once you started running towards the animal and chasing for the kill, you don't think at all but your focus was on the kill. You were completely immersed in the present moment, which is what meditation helps to achieve.

The practice of meditation can reduce anxiety, make you more confident, and give you the ability to calibrate in the moment. If you're working in a real-time environment where you have to make decisions in the moment such as the stock market or live sales, you must be present to the moment. If you're stuck in your head, your thoughts will take over and you won't be able to engage with your work.

Meditation only takes 15-20 minutes a night and all one needs is an alarm clock. Set the alarm clock to 15 minutes, sit down, close your eyes and focus on your breath. You will feel the presence sipping in within 5 minutes, and 15 minutes out, you'll feel complete presence. Once a person has meditated for months, they can naturally invoke this feeling.

2) Shift Your Prefrontal Cortex

The prefrontal cortex is a part of the brain located above the eyes responsible for controlling focus. The prefrontal cortex controls focus by identifying focus points for the brain and using the senses. Once the pre-frontal cortex is "focused" on something, it can keep the focus for a very long time. You might think it's your brain that does the focusing, but it's actually a tiny bit of the brain located at the very tip that controls your focus and you can optimize it.

The pre-frontal cortex is an evolutionary reaction to humans living in the wild, when a wild creature could attack and eat you. In response, the prefrontal cortex immediately focused on the threat and made us aware we're in immediate danger. It also helped us hunt and reproduce. The prefrontal cortex has largely remained the same, but now people are trying to alter it in order to optimize their focus at work. Even popular focus drugs such as Adderall work by alternating the prefrontal cortex.

The fastest way to shift the prefrontal cortex is to force your brain to do a hard task. If you start the activity, the prefrontal cortex finds ways to maintain it. It doesn't automatically activate when you want it, but you have to force it to activate. Want to go running but your brain won't do it? Go out and start running, and your prefrontal cortex will give you the focus to finish the exercise. Want to work on your big project? Start doing it and your prefrontal cortex will supply you with the focus and energy you need.

3) Love the Process

If you learn to love the process that gets you success, you will automatically get success. Many people are results-oriented and try to fast-forward to the end point instead of focusing on the daily process that gets them the success. This is because we live in an age of social media where people flash cars, travel destinations, and champagne. As a result, people believe that success is only about the end point and not the journey. Understand that the tiniest action you take today will have repercussions 30 days later. If you step out of your house to go to the gym, you won't see any results tomorrow but you will in 30 days later in the mirror.

Watch your steps on the way to the gym and praise yourself because you're already successful. Those tired slow steps that you take in the night, that's real success. You have to scale down your process and optimize your behavior for the small tasks that produce results. The process is essentially a set of daily milestones that you do that produce results when compounded. If you put in 30 minutes at the gym every night, you'll be fit in 1-2 months. If you work 10 hour shifts every day, you'll be successful at work. Making the tiny psychological shift that each daily action matters and contributes to the big picture will help you push through the last bit of resistance you have.

4) Optimize for Delayed Gratification

Daily Self-Discipline

Delayed gratification is about a long-term perspective. Success may take years. This is why one must prepare for long-term thinking and the sacrifices that follow. Gary Vaynerchuk, one of the leading media marketing CEOs spent a decade locked inside a room recording wine videos for his business. He didn't go out to parties or meetups. He honed his skill and knew that if he kept at it, his success would come even if it took 10 years of non-stop work.

A scientific experiment from the 70s targeting little children called the "Marshmallow Experiment" displays this. Children were given a marshmallow candy in front of them. If they ate it immediately, they only had that one, and if they waited longer, they were given two. Many children ate the candy right away while some waited and ate two candies. Later psychologists found that children who waited to eat two candies used to display higher problem-solving capability and had much better SAT scores.

5) De-Stress Periodically

De-stressing is the final follow-up to a successful work routine. One must take the time off to remove harmful toxins and reboot by taking the appropriate time off. If you're overworked, you're under constant stress and your body is filled with a stress chemical called cortisol. Cortisol is an evolutionary chemical that is responsible for external threats - if an animal attacks you, the body pumps you full of cortisol to put you on "alert" and make you more sensitive to the world. This makes you more likely to save your life when you're running away or trying to fight off an enemy (in an evolutionary sense).

The body can't differentiate between the modern world and the Caveman days, whereas if you're under constant stress from work it fails to recognize that you're in an office tower in New Jersey, and it pumps you full of that same chemical as if you were running away from a tiger. The effective way to de-stress is to completely remove yourself from your current environment. Book a flight to a beach, camp outdoors, go on a road trip, explore your city — do anything that doesn't revolve around your current environment. Once you de-stress, you can return to work recharged.

CHAPTER 3 – The Secrets of Goal-Setting

Have you ever looked in the mirror at your extra pounds and though "I should lose weight" but never took concrete action? Maybe you took action but give up after 2-4 weeks and reverted back to your old habits? Do you dream of quitting your soul-crushing 9-5 but never do it because you're too afraid of your boss? Are you stuck in a rut and see your life going nowhere? Is there an ambitious business idea lingering on your mind, but you delayed taking action for months or years? Most people think they should do it and they know they should take action. however, their daily routine prevents them from taking right action.

Goal-setting is about one thing: **Breaking your daily routine.**

The subconscious mind knows that if you take action, your life will change and it prevents you from doing so in order to chain you to your current regimen. You're a slave to a biological impulse. Your brain wants you to remain the same — this is a protective mechanism because it finds comfort in the familiar. Quitting your job, losing weight, starting a business — that's all unfamiliar so your mind will think of every excuse and rationalization in the book to keep you from changing. This is why you must set SMART goals that are time-sensitive and break your routine to get you to do what you need to do. Re-shaping your life begins at the goal-setting stage. If you set concrete goals, you'll be able to break your routine and start living the life you always wanted, one step at a time.

Start Now: "One Day" Never Comes

Remember the phrase: **"One day never comes."** You're only there when you take action. Have you held off your "big plans" for an imaginary date when you'll be ready? Are there ideas from 5 years ago that you haven't taken action on, but you told yourself you'll do them once you feel ready? Do you have a genius business idea that you never took action on because it's too complex? SMART goals exist to give you that last "push" that you need to kick yourself in the butt and take action. SMART goals are about breaking your routine and taking huge action towards your future goals. This chapter focuses on the goal-setting mindset that will push you directly into taking action.

How to Create SMART Goals for Better Output

Pro Tip: Goal-setting is like jumping into a pool. If you don't jump in immediately, you'll be tempted to stay on the sidelines where you don't get wet. If you actually jump in, you'll find the water is not too cold and you get used to the temperature fast. The same applies for SMART goals — you can take action immediately and complete the missing pieces on the way. You will never be ready until you take action, but once you take action, your brain will find ways to keep you moving. For example, if you quit your job with an abusive boss, you will start looking for a new job immediately and eventually land a better job.

SMART goals are the action plans you plan out before you take action. There is a distinction between SMART and HARD goals: SMART goals are incremental monthly small goals a person can achieve in a short time frame, while HARD goals are more long-term oriented and require deep-level identity change. S.M.A.R.T stands for:

→ **S-PECIFIC**

→ **M-EASURABLE**

→ **A-TTAINABLE**

→ **R-ELEVANT**

→ **T-IMELY**

Daily Self-Discipline

SMART goals separate empty promises such as "I need to lose weight" and concrete action-plans such as "I need to lose 50 pounds in 2 months." If you set concrete goals that have action-plans and deadlines, you'll be able to achieve them categorically instead of dabbling and hoping you get motivation by instinct. If you lack motivation, SMART goals set the foundation for change by taking daily small actions. SMART goals have to contain all of the following:

1) Specific

SMART goals must be specific. The technique of is to write concrete dates and times that you can follow-through by taking action. When you write down your goal, start by writing specifics: date, time, outcome, and any other details. The more specific you are the more concrete you can be about your action taking. If you want to lose weight, write how many pounds and how many weeks/months. If you want to get a raise, write by which month and by what percent of the salary. If you want to start a business, write by what date and how many dollar sales you want to make per month. If you want to quit smoking, write when you'll have your last smoke and what you plan to do afterwards.

A Harvard Business School professor once tasked his students to write down their life goals on a piece of paper. The students quickly returned their papers to the professor. The professor read every single piece of paper and disposed them into the trash in front of the class — except one. He took the last remaining paper and read it out loud; the paper said: "I want to get a 10% raise by September of next year." He singled that out as the best paper of the class because it set a concrete action plan and deadline – instead of vaguely claiming "I want to get promoted" the student claimed that she wanted "A 10% raise by September of next year." The single difference in specific goal and time is what differentiates a failed goal from a SMART goal!

2) Measurable

Remember the phrase: "**What gets measured gets managed.**" Goals can be measured in the same way we measure our living expenses. Do you know what your rent is at the end of each month, how much your bills are and how much you owe in taxes? Think of your goals as measurable units. If you want to be successful, measure the exact increase in money you need in order to finance your future life. Let's say "success" for you entails a house. an average house in the United States in somewhere in the range of $250,000. What would it take for you to obtain $250,000? Maybe you want to start a new business to obtain that money, or get a high-paying job. Whichever it is, what gets measured gets accomplished in advance.

You can measure your fitness progress the same - if you had abs at 16% body fat, you can measure how many pounds you need to lose to fall to that level of body fat. Once you have a general measurement, you can break down your goal into small daily measurements. For instance, if your goal is to lose 20 pounds in a month, your aim should be to lose 1 pound a day. Measure your weight every day to reassure that you're losing 1 pound a day, and this will reinforce your long-term goal.

3) Attainable

SMART goals have to be realistic and attainable based on your current situation. This is why the emphasis is placed on the short term. If you want to start a restaurant, you might be 1 or 2 years away from your goal. First, you need to get the funding for the restaurant. You'll likely have to work for at least a year before you can obtain the initial funding you need for the rent location, the food supplies, the chefs and the marketing. Goals have to be split into small attainable bits that stack on top of each other.

Pro Tip: Think of goals as laying bricks for a house. You lay one layer of bricks every week, and you repeat for a year. By the end of the year, you have a full house.

Back to our restaurant example: Make it your goal to work overtime for a year until you gather the initial funding. Split that year into goals for every month, and milestones you have to reach every week. Once you have small incremental milestones, you can start taking action right away. The actions will build on each other and in 1 year you'll have achieved your ultimate goal: to own a restaurant. If you just tell yourself "One day I'll get the funding for a restaurant," you will delay your goal indefinitely. If you change your life to optimize for the daily actions that would get you the funding, the mind shift alone will ensure you're successful in the long run.

4) Relevant

Ask yourself: Is this goal true to your heart? Do you want to set goals to impress others, or is this something you've always wanted to do for yourself? Set goals that provide personal fulfillment. You will burn out if you do it to satisfy others. SMART goals are about personal satisfaction because taking action is a lot easier once it's true to your heart.

For example, if you hate your major at university and set a goal to get better grades in school only to impress your parents - you'll likely fail because it's not true to your heart. However, if you make it your goal to switch majors and pursue something that's true to your heart, you will become a lot more eager to pursue your goals. SMART goals are about concrete action, but they're also about flipping your life on its head. If you're unsatisfied with your current situation, it's time to change everything.

5) Timely

Time sets the difference between a goal that gets done and a goal that gets missed! If you have no time-frames, you have no goals. Set specific time-frames and write deadlines for all goals, the most important of which is your start date. Once you have a start date, you know that your old life is about to change. If the goal requires a big life change such as quitting smoking, delay the start date until you feel confident you'll be able to maintain your new behavior. Specify the exact day you wish to start. It's not enough to say, "I'll start next month" or "I'll start in October." The right way is to say "I'll start on the 15th of October." Timing ensures your brain won't be able to think of excuses or procrastinate the date indefinitely. Once the date is written, it's set in stone.

How to Create HARD Goals for Higher Excellence

SMART goals force you to take action; HARD goals force you to change your identity. HARD goals are the ultimate level in goal-setting: They challenge your identity and help you re-shape yourself into the person you always wanted to be. The big distinction between SMART goals and HARD goals is that SMART goals can be broken down into daily goals, weekly goals or other small incremental goals - while HARD goals can only be worked on months or years in advance. HARD goals cut deep into your soul and question whether the action you're taking is true to your identity - and if not, to completely re-shape your identity as a person. Imagine SMART goals as the goals you take action on, and HARD goals as the goals that define you:

- **SMART goal: I want to start a business in 1 year.**
- **HARD goal: I want to be a successful business owner.**

HARD goals relate to who you are as a person: Are you a fitness-oriented person, are you an action-taker, do you aspire to be a doctor/business-owner/family person? HARD goals require deep-level identity change that might take years or even decades to materialize. this is why they're as essential as the SMART goals which we use to power through action-taking processes and momentum-building. HARD goals can re-enforce your identity if you're at a crossroads in life and you have a vision of who you want to become, but lack the directions to get there.

H.A.R.D goals stand for the following:

→ **H-EARTFELT**

→ **A-TTAINBLE**

→ **R-EQUIRED**

→ **D-IFFICULT**

1) Heartfelt

Is your HARD goal one that remains true to your ambitions, values and beliefs as a person? Are you setting your goal to only make money and please other people, or is this something you've always wanted to achieve since you were a kid? If your HARD goal is to start a business, are you doing it to impress your spouse/relatives/friends or is this something you always wanted to do yourself? Ask yourself: What were you born to do? Once you have an answer to that question, you will know if your goal was heartfelt or not. From there, you can start working on your goal or you can completely change your life itinerary.

Defining HARD goals is difficult because it cuts deep in your identity and questions whether the things you're doing are what you should be doing. Often, you will see ties to your past and how you got to where you are in life. Many times, people pursue goals that are not true to who they are, and they struggle because they're going against their nature. Heartfelt goals help you become fulfilled and not just successful. This is the highest level of goal-setting because you question whether the goals relate to your core desires or if you've been misled and taken off course by influences not true to your heart.

2) Attainable

The daily reality of work is different than the imaginary action plan we create. Imagine yourself as a Roman Emperor watching the gladiators battle. It looks easy from the chair, but once you're in the ring, it becomes a completely different ball game. The same applies to goals: the actions you take on a daily basis will be different to what you wrote down. This is why you have to be as realistic as possible, in order to minimize the difference between the goals you've set and the actions you're taking in real life.

For example, if your maximum work day is 10 hours, make sure to prepare your goals for the output a 10-hour day can generate in terms of income and productivity. Many times, our projected goals fall short of our actual daily output. You'll notice that you'll want to do less work, take more breaks, and experience more distractions. This is why you may have to adjust your goals for what you can realistically do based on your historic behavior. Know yourself and your capacity.

If you feel that you're slacking off, you should optimize to improve your performance. Your HARD goals have to be adjacent to your daily SMART goals. For example, if you only exercise 1 hour a day (your SMART goal) you can't expect to become a professional bodybuilder (your HARD goal). However, if you exercise 5-10 hours a day, you can suddenly become a competitive bodybuilder after a year. The small action-steps you take on a daily basis have to be aligned to your HARD goals and big-picture perspective.

3) Required

HARD goals must be critical. They can't be a mere formality. A HARD goal has to be critical to your existence, and you must feel an immediate urge to act on a HARD goal. It has to be tied deep in your core being, or they're not worth pursuing. Ask yourself: What is itching you right now that you're not acting on? Do you have a business idea and see people opening similar businesses that you could do better than them? Is this weighing on your soul deeply? If so, you must take action.

Are you worried that you'll miss out on Bitcoin if you don't invest now? Are you worried someone will take your business idea if you don't do it now? If the HARD goal is time-sensitive and you're feeling a deep urge to act on it right now, this is something you should pursue. If you want to pursue a formality, it's definitely not a HARD goal. For example, moving out of your neighborhood to a better neighborhood is a SMART goal, but is it really a HARD goal that challenges your core identity? It's not. A HARD goal is something that changes who you are, and challenges your currently worldview on what you deem possible.

4) Difficult

If the goals aren't difficult, they're not worth pursuing. If you can get something done without changing your whole life, you must think bigger! Ask yourself: What is the hardest thing you can do right now? The task that will require the most mental energy, the longest hours at work, and the most sacrifice on your end — this is what your HARD goal should be. HARD goals are meant to be difficult and challenge your very being, in order to trigger the change that you want to extract out of life.

Avoid setting medium-difficulty goals such "lose 10 pounds of fat" or "get a promotion at work" — those are SMART goals. The right approach to setting hard goals is to aim for the top. How can you become the fittest you've ever been in your life and reach your genetic potential at the gym? How can you find the highest paying job in your industry and work for the largest corporation? How can you start a profitable corporation and become one of the most successful brands in the world?

This is a difficult task, one that might require 5 or 10 years of perseverance, but that gives your life meaning in the grand scale. A truly difficult task will challenge your existence, make you question your course in life and ultimately allow you to become what you've always dreamed to become.

Exercise: To define your HARD goals, ask yourself the following questions and write the answers down on a piece of paper:

- Where do I want to be in 5 years?
- What do I intend to do about it?
- What am I afraid to miss out on in life?
- What do I plan to do about this?
- What change will that require from me?

The answers to those questions will give you insight in terms of your real, heartfelt long-term goals. Once you have the answers written down, you can cross-reference whether your HARD goals stand for the values listed above.

The Secrets to Turning Your Goals into Achievable Steps

Have you decided on goals you're stuck at the starting point but you don't know where to start? Are you too overwhelmed with the goal-setting process, and are the multiple goals you've set confusing you? Do you have a big "bucket list" to check off and you don't know how to prioritize your goals? Goal-setting can overwhelm a person because they're making too many changes at once. If your work occupies half of your day, and you're tired at the end of the day, how are you supposed to find the energy to exercise?

Let's say you want to start a business but you need $100,000 in inventory to start. Where do you get the investment money? What about bad habits and addictions? if you're trying to quit cigarettes, alcohol and drugs, how do you know when enough is enough? The wrong approach is to try to do everything at once — you will be overwhelmed. You might last for a few weeks, but then your motivation will dip. The right approach is to prioritize your goals, and act on each one individually until your actions are working in conjunction.

Most people lose motivation after 4 weeks. The biggest reason for that is that they set their goals too high and end up overwhelmed. For example, if someone tries to lose 20 pounds in 4 weeks, they might be successful during the first week using a starvation diet, but then they'll go right back to their old eating habits once their hunger kicks back in. The smarter approach for them would be to replace their foods with healthier ones, which will take longer than a starvation diet, but it's consistent.

If you set high expectations, your goal list is going to be full. This can be a negative because if you do too many things at once you will lose track of the meaning of those things. Prioritizing your goals and allocating your action steps gradually is critical. It's better to take on fewer goals that have more meaning to you, than many goals that have lesser meaning.

Goals can be converted to action steps with a simple 4-step process:

1) Don't Aim Too High

If you aim too high, you'll be disappointed if you don't make it. For example, if you aim to make $1 million dollars in 6 months or climb Mount Everest in 1 month, you'll likely fail. Set realistic goals based on your competency. If you're not competent, delay your goal until a point where you'll obtain the competency. If you want to climb Mt Everest, you won't be able to prepare for it in 1 month. However, if you prepare for a year in advance, there is a higher chance you'll be able to climb it given 12 months of practice.

If you want to become a millionaire, set it as a 5-year or a 10-year goal. This way you have enough time to develop and grow your business, or make it high up the corporate ladder. The right approach is to aim for moderate goals that you can achieve by preparing yourself and acting in small increments. If you aim too high, you will burn yourself out. The most effective measurement to prepare for realistic goals is to imagine an easy goal and double it.

Set goals based on evidence from the past. If you've lost 10 pounds in a month once, expect that you'll be able to repeat that. If you've made $100,000 in a year, you should be able to replicate that. In the former, it's wrong to aim for 50 pounds a month or $100,000 in a month instead of a year. Once you have evidence or a pattern you can use to judge your performance, you can plan in advance because your goals will be solidified by past evidence.

2) Limit the Number of Goals

Let's say you have 10 goals on your bucket list: 1) to move to another city 2) to lose 20 pounds 3) to quit smoking 4) to get a better job 5) to stop drinking 6) to travel to India 7) to meet a romantic partner 8) to learn the guitar 9) to wake up at 5 AM 10) to start meditating. Would those goals be realistic in 1 year? The answer is yes, but the sheer amount of goals would overwhelm you. The fact is that when you spread yourself out between dozens of goals, you won't know where to start and you will lose focus on the ones that matter.

Most people write down goals that are completely insignificant to their growth as a person — goals such as learning to play an instrument or waking up earlier. Significant goals are goals that propel you forward by helping you drop dead-weight such as addictions and help you make big moves such as finding a better job or starting a business. Limit the amount of goals you're setting by opting for a maximum of 3 goals a year - those goals should reflect your biggest desires.

3) Sort Goals by Priority

If you hate your body, make it your #1 goal to lose weight. If you're unsatisfied with your monetary situation, focus on finding a new job. If your health is suffering due to an addiction, make it your priority to quit your addiction. To prioritize goals, identify what would trigger the biggest change in your life. For instance, starting a business would make a far bigger difference than learning to play the guitar. Once you've cut down your goals to only 2-3 core goals that matter, you should sort them by your competency level.

Start with the goal that you're the most competent at, because this will build the leverage to proceed onto harder goals. If you have to choose between losing weight, finding a new job and dropping an addiction - start with whichever one you're the most confident you'll succeed at first: If you have previous fitness experience, start with weight loss. If you have experience switching jobs, find a new job first. If your bad habit is not a major part of your life, drop it first.

4) Chop Goals Down in Weekly Increments

Break down your goals in weekly increments, or small milestones that you can cross out weekly. Start by "zooming in" on your larger goal. If you have a goal that will take you 1 year to achieve, set smaller monthly milestones. Once you've set the monthly milestones, set weekly milestones that feed into your larger monthly milestones. This way you can exclusively focus your attention on your weekly output, and that weekly output will translate to gradual monthly output until you've reached your final yearly goal.

The way to be effective with large-scale goals that take a lot of time is to start small. Remember this: **"You are the culmination of your daily actions."** If you set a milestone for each week, and you carry out your tasks on the daily, consider yourself successful. This is because the weeks will compound and you'll eventually obtain your larger goals.

How to Reward Yourself for Progress

What if you're successful for 2 weeks, you take a break and you immediately fall back in old unhealthy habits? What if you quit smoking and go right back after 4 weeks? Are you worried that if you take a break, you'll lose momentum and all your hard work will be for nothing? Many people relapse on their bad habits when they're let off the hook - this is because they've been kept on a leash for weeks or months at a time, and start craving their old lifestyle. It's extremely difficult to change your ways, but to avoid burnout a person has to take some time off and reward themselves regularly. To reward yourself without slipping back into your old habits, it's important to plan out small "rewards" accordingly.

Logistics planning your rewards is the first step. For example, if you quit smoking and you want to celebrate that fact, it's better to book a holiday abroad instead of go to a party. Once you're on a holiday you'll be able to relax on a beach and soak in the fresh air, while a party you would be tempted you to go right back to your smoking habit. If you've changed your diet and you now only consume organic food, you have to be careful not to fall to the temptation of your old unhealthy ways of living.

Why Reward Yourself Now?

Rewarding yourself is useful for two reasons: 1) It reinforces that you're successful and crossed a certain milestone 2) It helps to avoid burnout at work. People who work hard will often times spend days entire locked inside their offices in order to work harder and increase productivity. If they do this for weeks at a time they risk "burnout", and essentially start losing motivation. To avert this process, there are many ways to break the chain by rewarding yourself temporarily; until you're fully recharged and you can go back to your work schedule. If you're celebrating a small milestone, start with a small celebration. If you've achieved big success you should consider taking more time off to reward yourself and maybe even take a whole month off.

Pro Tip: Rewarding yourself is not about posting on social media. Did you lose 5 pounds in a week? Did you stop eating junk food for a week? Did you quit smoking recently? These are worthy of celebration, but a reward has to fulfill you spiritually by showing you a new side of life, one that is not prone to external validation.

The following are the best ways to unwind and reward yourself after achieving a milestone:

1) Book a Weekend Holiday

Book a weekend holiday to a place that looks nothing like your office: The mountain, beach, lake — nature of any kind. Forget about the sound of computers and phones going off, and unplug yourself from modern society. If you've been working for weeks at time, your body is full of a stress chemical called cortisol. To flush it out of your system, you have to change your environment completely. Flights can be cheap and you can book a flight for your break in advance — both cheaper and motivating as you'll expect a reward while you're working.

It's possible to travel on a budget by flying with cheap airlines and staying in cheap housing or even house shares if you're young. Make your destination as different to your current place of work as possible. If you work in a busy place, make your destination a quiet place where you can sit and do nothing. Don't overdo it. Most times, 1-2 days at the beach is enough. Sit by the ocean and listen to the waves at night. Watch the stars. Take time to think about what you did in retrospect, and what future big projects are ahead of you. Try to meditate on your thoughts. This will free you of cortisol and recharge you. You will reward yourself by changing your environment and your brain will reinforce the fact that you're successful.

2) Create a Movie Night

Humans are social creatures. Historically, we evolved to live in 150-person tribes and millions of years of evolution we spent living closely to other people. This made us crave social activity, and engaging with people socially makes us more relaxed. If you're uncomfortable at parties due to high amounts of alcohol, a movie night is the perfect reward for you. Invite your closest friends and family for a movie or a Netflix comedy. Cook some popcorn and spend the night watching movies. If you've achieved a lot of success, you can even drink and order junk for the night. You've earned it. Finish your movie night off by preparing a nice late-night bubble bath with wine. This way you can socialize and relax, and then complete your relaxation with a long relaxing therapy bath.

3) Explore the City

Go out to your city and do the first activity you come across. Watch a football game, go see a tourist attraction, go to a bar, participate in a festival. If you live in a major city where there are activities going on around the clock. Cities are full of entertainment options that can provide you with fun activities around the clock. Do you miss your childhood days when you were carefree and driving go-karts? Go find one and invite your friend. This will make you feel carefree, and you can combine multiple activities at once. How about you see a new blockbuster at the cinema, and top your evening off with a trip to your favorite bar? Your city probably has many hidden attractions and areas that you can explore. If you don't want to spend money, you can just walk and listen to music. Walking is a very meditative activity because it allows you to soak in the energy of the city.

4) Buy Yourself a Gift

Pretend it's your birthday and get yourself something you always wanted but didn't have the courage to purchase because you were conservative with your money. Did you want to get one of the new iPhones for a while, but held off from purchasing them? Reward yourself by buying a new phone. Go to your favorite book store and purchase a new book. Take a trip to the department store and try out a new pair of jeans. Go pick up a new pair of Nikes. Old-school consumerism can relax you. Appeal can make you feel new and refresh your sense of fashion. Whatever you've been missing out on, reward yourself by buying an item that you always wanted.

4 Ways to Create a Goal-Friendly Environment

Do you live in a loud household where you can't get anything done because the noises interrupt you? Are your neighbors noisy and interrupting you constantly while you're trying to get work done? Is your desk cluttered and disorganized and you struggle to organize your belongings? The environment you reside in will have repercussions on your productivity - the same as the people influencing you.

Bruce Lee used to say "If you put water into a cup, it becomes the cup. If you put water into a bottle, it becomes the bottle." In other words, you are a product of your environment. What happens when your environment is sub-par and preventing you from achieving your peak productive potential? It's time to clean house. This can mean organizing your current living space, or it could mean completely replacing your space by moving into a new neighborhood. The physical environment in which you reside in will dictate your energy output. To make the most out of your energy, you have to live in the kind of environment that is organized for productivity.

The following 4 techniques will help you create a goal-friendly environment:

1) Clean Your Room

Daily Self-Discipline

To become productive, you have to minimize your office space to only the essential tools you need: The desk, chair, computer and/or any other tools necessary for the job. Dump everything else in the trash. If your environment is cluttered with food, boxes from eBay orders, electronics, clothes and other messy things - this will reflect in your productivity because you'll be constantly distracted by everything around you. The same applies for your computer: clear out your desktop and put every distracting icon such as games and music into a separate folder.

Only allow the most critical software on your desktop. If your room is dirty, take a full day to clean it and dispose of any items that aren't critical to your productivity. Give your old clothes away to the Red Cross. Make sure you have freedom to move your hands and that you're sitting in a forward position if you're working at an office. Your back will be exhausted from 10-hour shifts and you must give it adequate support. Once you've removed all unnecessary items and your room is clean, you'll be ready to start producing.

2) Move to a Different Area

Do you live with in an area that is too loud and distracting? If you answered yes, move out. The difference in productivity you'll experience will make up for the loss of living in a rent-free environment. Find a new apartment in a peaceful area where you can focus 100% on your work. This will enable you to minimize all distractions and maximize productivity. Moving out is a radical tactic, as many people sign contracts for rental properties that expire after 6 months or a year. However, the increase in productivity is worth it effort.

Move out even if your interior living situation is ideal but the area is too harmful to your goals. If you live in a central area of the city where bars play loud music at night, this will affect your sleep. Aim to live in an area that is suitable to your goals. For example, if you want to lose weight and you live in an area with many bakeries and fast-food joints, move to a place where there are health food stores and jogging paths. This way, you can exercise and purchase good food instead of being tempted by unhealthy food.

3) Cut Off Bad Influences

If some people such as your love partner or even your parents are holding you back by interrupting your schedule, cut them off. Our habits are formed by the people we surround ourselves with, and if the people closest to you are not aligned with your goals this can create inconvenience for both of you. It's wise to break contact with people temporarily to see if they make a difference. For example, if you're staying in your parent's place to save money but you are made to feel like a nuisance, it's better to move out. Your productivity will increase once you're free to work in your own living space. If you have friends with bad habits who influence you directly or indirectly, cut them off until you drop your bad habits and they can no longer influence you. Sometimes you can end relationships temporarily and re-start them once you've gained ground on your productivity.

4) Go to a Goal-Friendly Environment

Modern society has living spaces and environments that cater to goal-oriented people. The most notable examples include meditation clubs and co-working spaces. Co-working spaces are a relatively new invention for creative people who want to network together while they're working. A person can join a co-working space by purchasing a membership card similar to a gym. This allows them to network with like-minded individuals and focus when they need to work. There are many clubs such as meditation clubs where a person can learn a new skill and organize with individuals who are familiar with the practice. If you can't create a goal-friendly environment, you can join an existing one directly.

Chapter 4 - Techniques to Amp Up Output

Transform Your Life with the Getting Things Done (GTD) Method

Do you forget small things? Have you reminded yourself you need to get something done the whole day and then ended up forgetting about it? One day at work your boss tasks you to bring a business paper to work. You go back home and become paranoid: Your mind thinks, "Get that business paper" while you're eating, your start thinking of business papers when you're petting your dog, you go for a jog thinking about business papers at night, you almost trip on the stairs thinking about business papers, and in bed you lay awake at 3 AM thinking about the business papers.

The next morning, what happens? You get distracted by the news of the conflict in Syria, you see your dog made a mess in the kitchen, your wife starts telling you about unpaid bills — and what is the last thing you think of? The business papers. That's right, you forgot. A very popular technique that helps you remember and organize your life is the GTD method by David Allen.

The "Get Things Done" (GTD) method was invented by productivity consultant David Allen, an expert in productivity consulting with over 30 years of experience. The book became one of the most iconic and best-selling productivity books of all time. The GTD method is a 5-step method that focuses on writing down everything related to the mind, removing the unnecessary, and converting "actionable" and "unactionable" thoughts into appropriate "work tasks."

GTD is not for everyone — this is a system for people who have time to consider everything and wish to take control over their life by re-evaluating their life decisions. Example: Your boss tasks you to bring business papers at work. What is your "reminder" here? It's to bring business papers. The GTD method explains that the "reminder" has to be removed from your head by writing it down. You basically convert it to an "action item" on your big paper. We can effectively convert all planned tasks into action items and organize them down by priority. This shifts our attention from thinking about reminders to do to actually taking actionable steps. The GTD technique focuses on important tasks, so all tasks that require less than 2 minutes to complete shouldn't be written down.

The GTD Technique is a 5-step process:

Step 1: Capture

Step 2: Clarify

Step 3: Organize

Step 4: Reflect

Step 5: Engage

How it works: The GTD technique is based on taking note all your "incompletes" (things you have to do), then deciding if the "incompletes" are 1) "actionable" (ones you take action on) or 2) "unactionable" (ones you can't do anything about) and then taking action by focusing on the most important work items you've written down. The GTD technique requires a complete "brain dump" in order to jot down everything that preoccupies your mind.

Daily Self-Discipline

Once you've completed your brain dump, you have to split the incompletes in 2 ways: actionable and unactionable. The unactionable incompletes are discarded, while the actionable ones are prioritized based on which one has the highest impact on your life and productivity. The GTD method requires a lot reflection and can't be done in a single sitting. You must be prepared to spend at least a few hours reflecting about things that occupy your mind, writing each thought down and deciding which one would have the most impact on your life.

Step 1 - Capture

The first step of the GTD method is to write down what preoccupies your brain. Effectively we're trying to complete a "brain dump" and writing everything that finds its way to our brain. It doesn't matter if the thoughts are related to work, family, business or the weather. What matters is that if something is on your mind it must to be written down. The thoughts can be of big, small, medium importance. They can be of personal, professional or other nature — write them all down. Get a piece of paper and write down 100% of everything that preoccupies your mind. This process can take a while because the average human has hundreds of thoughts, but we usually spin the same 40-50 thoughts on a daily basis and those should be written down. Write down even items that are not related to your work.

Example: Let's say you have a mole on your face that affects your self-confidence and you want visit a laser mole removal clinic. Write that down. Let's say you plan to travel to India and you've had this on your mind for years. Write that down. Let's say you're about to start a new business and you don't know how to get distributers for your product. Write that down. Dump everything — take your time and don't rush this. Imagine if an Alien species descended from another galaxy and scanned your entire brain – what would they find? Do that for yourself but only write down what's on your mind. Get your thoughts out on a piece of paper.

Step 2 - Clarify

Your brain dump should have at least solid 50 thoughts written down - proceed by sorting them into "actionable" and "unactionable" items. The difference is that for one you can take action and for another you can't do anything. Simply assign an arrow to each thought on the right and classify it as "actionable" or "unactionable." How do you know the difference? If you have a thought about how you got rejected by your high school crush, this is "unactionable" - you can't get a time machine and go back in time. If your thought was about how you need to lose 10 pounds in 3 weeks - this is "actionable." File it under "actionable" and move on.

Once you've assigned a full list of "actionable" and "unactionable" items - discard the unactionable items into the trash. This will leave only the actionable ones on the table - those are actions that you should dedicate your life on. Focus on removing the unactionable items from your head because they hinder your productivity and rob you of your mental energy.

Step 3 - Organize

You're now left with actionable items - items that you can take concrete action on. To proceed, you must sort the actionable items into items that you can achieve in the immediate future and actions that you have to delay over the long-term. This is based on your competency and time necessary to achieve the action steps.

Example: If your actionable item is to open a bookstore, you might have to delay it in favor of daily work that would allow you to save the finances necessary to open the bookstore. Both thoughts are actionable, but one takes requires more time and effort. This is why you have to prioritize your actionable plans based on which one you can do first. You can split these down to daily, weekly, monthly and yearly action-steps. The yearly actions should reflect your long-term goals while your weekly and daily actions should be updated based on the work and projects that come up daily — those are more dynamic.

Step 4 - Reflect

Micro actionable steps will require weekly changes because your weekly life is dynamic. While many large actionable steps are clear-cut and require longer commitment, the ones we handle on a daily basis will change based on circumstance. Let's say you want to save $20,000 in a year — you can't do much about this immediately. However, you can focus on making $500 a week which would ultimately lead you to saving $20,000 in a year.

If you focus on saving $500 a week, there will be daily and weekly tasks you have to accomplish in order to achieve this. For instance, you may need to increase your productivity on the daily and you must write down your actionable steps for the small weekly goals that you set, which ultimately lead to a larger goal. Take each week to review your goals and change them to ensure you remain on the right path.

Step 5 - Engage

The final step and the most crucial one — once you've completed your "brain dump," you've organized your action-steps and you have a weekly plan, all that remains is to take concrete action. Keep a weekly list of action steps that you must take action on. This will clear your brain because it's not affected by things that are unactionable, and you can focus 100% on the actionables that affect your life. Schedule weekly revisions and add new actions as your projects change, but remember to reevaluate and take a step back every 2-3 months in case you have new priorities and occupations. This will ensure that you're always on top of your life and that you're completely organized in the way you go about productivity.

Achieve More with the Pomodoro Technique

Do you burn out at work doing a 30-minute task and end up slacking off on social media? Do you maybe do 2-3 tasks in a single burst of energy and then you've had enough? Do you want to die when your boss focuses you to do multiple things at once, and you can't seem to get even one done? Many people start taking up "focus" pills and end up addicted to prescription drugs.

Even those who work from home struggle with productivity. We've all been there! The second you have to work, suddenly you also have to take a shower, have a cup of coffee, listen to that new song, clean your dirty room - anything to avoid doing the actual work. We really believe that we must do those things, but deep down we know we're procrastinating. If you're a "perfectionist" you will struggle with this even more because you set standards for yourself and it takes you hours to actually start doing something and even then, you end up with minimal output at the end of the day.

How do you get over this? The answer: Split your day into pomodoros with little breaks in between.

The brain has a limited capacity. It can't focus on a single task for an entire day and requires periodical breaks. Unfortunately, most believe that to be successful they have to do an 8-hour stint of non-stop work during the work day. This is reason modern society is addicted to prescription pills that alter our brain chemistry, and even students are taking up Adderall to focus on studies. Since altering your brain chemistry is unhealthy, the right way is to account for the brain's natural desires to relax after focusing, and to plan out a productive day in advance by anticipating the work-break balance. It's entirely possible to create your own schedule that allows you to focus on small tasks for 45 minutes and then take breaks between sessions to avoid burnout. The technique that focuses on becoming productive for a certain amount of time and then following that up with a periodic break is the "Pomodoro Technique."

Pomodoro: 25-Minute Work Sessions to Success

The Pomodoro technique is a famous productivity technique pioneered by Francesco Cirillo, an Italian chef who discovered that by observing his clock for 25 minutes and then taking a break, he was able to cook more and make better meals for his clients at the restaurant. He had a tomato-shaped kitchen timer that he used to work with.

Cirillo broke his sessions down into manageable 25-minute work bursts that he called "pomodoros," following up each burst with a short break (3-5 minutes) for relaxation. He didn't do this the whole day, but once he completed 4 pomodoros, he took a longer 30-minute break.

The Pomodoro Technique is a brain technique that optimizes your brain for work output but then relaxes it to avoid burnout. This follows a natural cycle that responds to our evolutionary nature. When we used to hunt in the wilderness millions of years ago, we would usually find an animal, struggle to kill it and then take a break. We didn't run around with spears 24/7. Our brain has to receive periodic breaks in order to preserve clarity and sanity. Ideally those breaks can be optimized after 25-minute work increments, followed up by 5-minute breaks and a 30-minute break after 4 successful pomodoros.

How Pomodoro Works: An Average Day

Daily Self-Discipline

The easiest way to imagine an average day on the Pomodoro technique is to break your day down into 4 or 5 full pomodoros (2 hours each) that you scratch off — one full pomodoro takes 2 hours because it's split in 4 25-minute mini pomodoros and breaks. Once you've done 6 full pomodoros, consider your work day successful. 4 full pomodoros correspond to an average 8-hour work day.

For example, start with one mini Pomodoro when you wake up. Take 25 minutes to work, then 5 minutes off, and repeat this 3 more times. This should take you a total of 2 hours. Once you're done, scratch one full pomodoro off your list. Take 30 minutes off, catch some air, listen to a song and do the opposite of what you did — disengage.

When you work you must be 100% engaged with the task for maximum productivity, but once you're on break you want to do the opposite and allow your brain to recover without adding any pressure. Once you've done your first pomodoro and taken a longer 30-minute break, repeat the process 2 or 3 more times before you stop for lunch. You'll effectively have 3-4 full pomodoros completed by lunch time – this is a solid 6 hours of work in the morning. Come lunchtime, take 1 hour off to fully recover. Follow that up by completing 2 more pomodoros - this will optimize your day for at least 8 hours of work. If you wish to work a 10-hour day or even a 15-hour day, you can add 2-3 extra pomodoros to your day.

The 4 Rules of Pomodoro

1. Activities Shouldn't Require More Than 4 Pomodoros

If your activity requires more than 4 pomodoros (that is in essence over 8 hours of work) you should break it down into small actionable steps. For instance, if you have to deliver a PowerPoint presentation with 50 slides and 10 slides take you around 2 hours to complete, you should split that activity into 4 full pomodoros. This way you will complete half of the slides in 2 full pomodoros. You can't sneak in more work on your Pomodoro as this goes against the rules - once the 25 minutes are out, you must take a 5-minute break or a 30-minute break appropriately. All large tasks that require more time than is given should be broken down into small 25-minute pomodoros. Find out how much time your activities require in advance in order to optimize your pomodoros.

2. Pomodoros Must Be Protected From Interruptions

All internal and external interruptions have to be removed for a pomodoro to be considered legitimate. You can't work for 15 minutes and then browse Facebook or talk to a colleague at work. Optimally you should be focused at 100% during your pomodoro and be located in an environment that encourages productivity. Prepare your environment by minimizing clutter, removing unnecessary items and distancing yourself from influences that distract you from work, whether those are the Internet, people or any other distraction. Focus during your pomodoro to protect your productivity.

3. Recaps Count as Work Under Pomodoros

You are allowed to recap and review your work during a pomodoro because this relates directly to your productivity. Example: If you're a chef at a restaurant and you're at the end of your work day, you need to take the time to write down ingredients to shop for the next day, how much you need of x ingredient, how many pastries you need to bake and more. This helps you organize your day. This is also counted under productivity and it can be measured under a single pomodoro. If you recap and review your work, this is also considered work under pomodoro rules.

4. Optimize Pomodoros for Personal Objectives

Optimize your pomodoros to take actions that create value in return. In essence, the only time we get value is when we produce value in return. This means that to make more money and to get promoted at work, you must increase the quality of your output. How do you do that? By focusing all your attention on the little work tasks that enable you to increase your output. Most people spend 30-40% of their work day actually working - the rest is spent dwelling on work, being distracted or doing nothing at all. If you only optimize your work day to work at 80% capacity with the time given, you can double your productivity and increase your revenues by a huge margin.

4 Productive Habits of the Zen-to-Done Method

Do you struggle keeping your day-to-day habits? Do you delay your "productive" habits indefinitely and end up doing half of what you're supposed to be doing? Organizing yourself can be exhausting and confusing because we're overwhelmed by influences from the external world, and it's hard to "tune out" and focus on what's really important. We're bombarded with stimulation on social media that encourages us to go down the route of least resistance and even the opposite is true — productivity habits can clog our mind because there are too many of them and we don't know which one is the best or where to start. The "Zen To Done" Method is the most simplified and minimalistic productivity method that optimizes productivity for 4 basic habits that you do on the daily. This method was developed by Leo Babauta of "Zen Habits" in order to break a day down into step-by-step habits based on individual goals.

The Human Element of Productivity

There is a human element to productivity — we cannot function like robots that work for 30-40 minutes and then shut off consistently. In reality, we constantly experience peaks and dips of productivity, we feel a surge of energy and then we feel a diminishing of energy. Some days we're on top of the world and we can work without stopping and other days we're all out of energy and can't seem to get anything done. The question is: How do we gain consistency? If the human element prevents us from acting the same way every day and popular techniques can't work with consistency - what is the right approach?

The ZTD approach accounts for the human element by focusing on broad behavioral patterns. ZTD focuses on behaviors that can be replicated on a daily basis, irrespective of your mood or energy levels. The ZTD method begins by analyzing your broader plans, effectively mapping out your long-term and short-term goals and then focusing on scheduling action-steps that you can do on a daily basis that produce the results you're after.

The 4 Habits of "Zen To Done" Method

The original Zen To Done method featured 10 habits, but the minimalist ZTD method (which is most popular) is comprised of 4 core habits:

ZTD Habit #1: Collect

The ZTD technique focuses on letting out all ideas in one piece of paper: Making a brain dump by writing down everything that's on your mind. If you have business ideas left to accomplish, write them down. If you have things that you'd like to improve such as your health or bad habits, write down all of them. There shouldn't be any difference between quitting your smoking habit and starting a business — both are action steps you must do and they should be written down. Take out a piece of paper or open a note on your computer and write down all your goals and things you plan to get done this year.

Dedicate one page for your goals and another page for action plans that you will need to obtain those goals. Take your time as the first habit is the most crucial — it might take you hours to remember all the things you've wanted to do and things which bother you on a daily basis. If you're poor and want to take action steps to become wealthy, write that down. If you're out of shape and plan to become fit, write it down. If you're addicted to a substance and want to quit, write that down. Write down everything.

Pro Tip: To find what to write down, go for a walk late at night and let your mind unwind. Play music and let thoughts come into your head naturally. Once you have those thoughts, write them down on your phone. This is better than "forcing" your brain to come up with things to do while you're locked at home.

ZTD Habit #2: Process

Once you've successfully written down everything, it's time to convert your thoughts into daily action steps you can follow up on. Example: If your goal is to lose 20 pounds you will likely have to take multiple actions - you'll have to exercise, replace your nutrition, drink more water, de-stress, etc. To accomplish all those things at once you'll have to write down what you would have to do in an average day. Maybe you have to wake up earlier to exercise in the morning - write that down. Maybe you have to purchase gym equipment and learn how to cook healthy food - write that down. At night, if you plan to run and lift weights at the gym - write that down. In essence you have to write down the new habits that would be required of you each day in order to achieve your long-term goals.

ZTD Habit #3: Plan

Once you've written down your daily action plans and new habits, it's important to revise your action-plans based on the things you've accomplished. What we plan for and what we do in real life is a lot different. For example, we might plan to run for 30 minutes at night but our energy levels dip after 10 minutes when we actually attempt it. This is why we have to optimize to progressively ramp up the exercise by running 5 minutes more every week. This way in 4 weeks we can actually achieve a 30-minute run, once our physical condition improves. The same practice applies to productivity at work - progressively increase your work load and update your action plans based on your performance.

ZTD Habit #4: Do

Once you've planned everything - DO, DO, DO! It all comes down to action. You've removed the clutter from your head, you've written down your goals and now you have to take the actions that produce the results. Start by scheduling when you're going to do a certain action down to the hour. Example: Set your alarm clock to 5 AM and wake up early for your work. Set milestones you want to achieve by mid-day. Update your accomplishments every day and edit your action plans accordingly. Once you're actually engaged with your daily tasks, you become "self-aware" in terms of with how much work you can take on and you can increase your performance progressively in order to ramp up your output.

How to Keep Track of Productivity?

The computer. Write down your daily and weekly to-dos on a list on your computer. This is ideal if you're working from home or rely on your computer for work. You can edit your plans according to the changes in your life. Many times, we need to alter our goals once we hit milestones, and your action plan will require constant editing. The computer is the best place to do this.

Smartphone apps. Find a memo app that allows you to write down your action steps, or one that has daily reminders in case you forget something. Use the alarm clock to remind you when to take a certain action step. If you run at 10 PM each night, set an alarm clock for 9:30 PM. This way, you have 30 minutes to prepare yourself for your run, both physically and mentally.

Using the "Don't Break the Chain" Technique for Consistency

Do you manage to stay on track with a goal and can keep the habit for one month, three months or even half a year but then your output is unsatisfactory? Do you struggle increasing your yearly output and you're stuck at the same salary level for years, when you know what you need to do to increase your earnings? Do you wonder why this happens to you while your acquaintances progress?

The answer is simple: You're not doing enough. Even if you're consistent, chances are you're wasting a day or two every week and you're not maximizing your time for productivity. Consistency is a giant problem for people trying to reinvent themselves. Despite the initial "push," our biology eventually wires us to crave stability. Unless we assume our new habits as part of our identity, we eventually slip back into our old way of living. The bigger problem is when we think we're consistent, but we end up wasting days that we could spend productively. How do we not break the chain? We use every day.

Solution #1: Using Every Day in a Year

Reevaluate your off days: Even if you're killing it at work and you're satisfied with your daily performance, you should still be aware of the time lost. Let's you've kept up your work habit for a year — you've been working on your dream but you still haven't achieved your desired goal. The solution: Work every day in the year. We're given 365 days a year. If you work 5 days a week, you might think you're consistent but zoom out and take a big-picture perspective — you're losing 8 days a month or almost 100 days a year. The lost weekends add up, and once you lose 8-10 days a month due to off-days and holidays, you're robbing yourself of 100+ days you could have spent working and increasing your productivity. That's almost 1/3 of the year wasted.

Solution #2: Work as If You're Being Audited

If you want to boost your productivity on the daily, implement this one trick: Work as if you're being audited. This is a huge mental habit that trains your brain to utilize every minute for productivity. Most people work 2-3 hours in an average 8-hour work day — the rest is spent browsing the internet, talking to colleagues, sitting in the lounge or doing nothing. If your work solely relies on the output — that is, your income is measured based on the product you produce and not the time spent — you must utilize this technique to produce more in the time given.

Example: Take a look at your day. If someone audits your day the same way they audit your finances, what will they discover? Have you spent every minute of your work day working, or were you slacking off on the internet? Did you take breaks that lasted longer than your work sessions? Identify your problem and fix it immediately. If you apply a rigid and thorough auditing on your daily performance, you will discover areas where you need to improve in and double your productivity.

The "Don't Break the Chain" Method

This is a reliable method for not breaking consistency and making use of every day in the year. This method is for the hardest performers who want to make a big change in their life and assume a completely new identity that re-shapes their life and prepares them for the future. The method was popularized by comedian Jerry Seinfeld, one of the biggest names in stand-up comedy and TV. Mr. Seinfeld struggled with consistency as his job commanded him to do perform in front of audiences weekly, and he invented a trick that helped him become productive every day of the year.

How it works: Take a big calendar with each day in the year, and mark the days you've worked with a giant X. You will soon realize that if you take weekends off, almost a quarter of the days each month will be left unmarked. Start marking each day you've spent working and only mark "X" on the dates if you've successfully completed all your tasks for the day. This way you'll feel inclined to increase your productivity on your off-days and prepare yourself for month-to-month consistency. This method is the final elevation in productivity because it's designed for people who want to make every day count and are ready to immerse themselves fully. If you're actively pushing yourself and productivity becomes a routine, you can use the "Don't Break The Chain" method to implement a chain of productivity that will get you what you want out of life: a higher salary, better fitness/health, more business success, and healthy relationships.

4 Science-Backed Hacks for Increased Productivity

University studies and research facilities have carried out studies that relate certain activities to productivity. Exercising, sleeping better, and walking were linked to a significant increase in productivity and the same can impact willpower in significant proportions.

Remember the saying, "What you eat is what you are"? In essence, what we consume and how we treat our bodies reflects in our mental performance. If we supply our body with the right nutrients and physical exercise it craves, it will give us mental clarity and higher performance at work. To start a life-changing process, you must start by optimizing your health and then applying the numerous productivity habits that exist. The following scientific studies prove that certain activities are linked to an increase in productivity:

1. Exercise Improves Productivity

The largest study that correlated exercise to productivity was carried out at Bristol University in the UK. The university took 200 employees and assigned exercise days and no-exercise days the same people. They observed the behavior of each individual on both days and analyzed how their performance. After the tested participants were analyzed, their results were calculated, and this is what the study revealed:

- 21% increase in concentration
- 22% increase in finishing work on time
- 25% higher ability to work without taking breaks
- 41% increase in motivation to work.

Why is exercise linked to productivity? The act of exercise is not a magic pill, but the mind reflects the condition of the body. We evolved to live out in nature and most of us were fit because we had to hunt for food and we spent our days outdoors. If we're fit, we're able to sleep less, concentrate more and we feel motivated to do more. If we're not fit, we experience constant mood swings, lack of motivation/focus and inability to stay consistent at work.

This is why improving your fitness can make a dramatic impact in your output at work. This study determined that exercise in itself increases productivity by almost 25%. Taking into account that the study was carried out on people with little/no prior exercise experience, it is safe to say that people who make fitness a part of their daily schedule will be able to perform mental tasks at 50-100% higher capacity than people who do not exercise at all.

Stanford University carried out a study that proved the benefit of walking for idea-generation. Two research professors analyzed people who were sitting and people who were walking for effects on productivity and idea-generation. The study found that people who practice walking on a daily basis experience a 60% increase in unique responses to stimuli and generate more unique ideas.

2. Sleep Improves Productivity

If you're sleep-deprived, you're likely to perform worse at work and experience low attention retention compared to people who received a full night's sleep. The minimum amount of sleep a person should have is 8 hours a night - this is optimal as it allows us to recharge. Sleep increases performance, boosts alertness and replenishes our energy. There were two notable studies that prove sleep can increase productivity.

The largest study from the American College of Occupational and Environmental Medicine determined that employees at the college who suffered from insomnia were spending thrice as much time on tasks, compared to employees who had a full night's sleep. Employees who suffered from lack of sleep were found to be less motivated to perform tasks, experienced severe lack of focus and had trouble remembering things. Sleep is tied to all mental performance:

Endurance, focus and consistency. If we go without adequate sleep, we are diminishing our performance abilities by a significant margin.

Varn Bexter and Steve Kroll Smith conducted a scientific study in a corporate environment that analyzed the effect on taking power naps. Employees who took power naps at work were more alert at the job tasks and experienced increases in productivity. Employers are now encouraging their workers to take power-naps at work in order to increase their performance.

3. Music Boosts Productivity

Music is tied to increasing positive stimulus in the brain and idea-generation. A study conducted at University of Miami determined that people who listen to music at work tend to generate faster output, better ideas and had a positive mood compared to people who didn't listen to music at work. The appropriate music might vary, as certain songs can be distracting and if you use music to boost your productivity you should be careful in order to pick a record that boosts your mood without distracting you from the job at hand.

4. Green Offices Boost Productivity

Recently a study at the University of Exeter in England analyzed the impact that plants have on employees in the work space. The study was split in two groups: One group worked out of offices without green plants and another worked out of offices furnished with green plants. The study determined that people who work surrounded by plants experience a 15% increase in productivity and reduced stress levels. Humans evolved to live in forests as trees provide us with natural shade. It's no wonder most of us feel at peace when we're surrounded by plants.

Chapter 5 - Planning for Daily Success

6 Morning Routines to Start the Day on Top

Do you feel productivity highs and lows? One day you wake up productive and ready to work, and another you feel sluggish and don't feel like working at all. Ever wonder why the morning is the hardest part of the day to start working? The morning sets the tone for productivity — if you start off productive early in the morning, you'll likely keep up your productivity throughout the day. If you start off feeling lazy, chances are you won't get anything done the whole day.

Mornings are detrimental to success because the first 3 hours in the morning are when mental energy peaks. The first 2-3 hours upon waking up is when we experience peak mental clarity. This is why you must set the tone of your day in the first 3 hours! If you miss out on this short time frame, you will feel decaying mental energy throughout the day and your productivity will amount to zero. Mornings set the tone for what we do throughout the day, while evenings only prepare us for the next day. This begs the question: How do you feel consistently motivated in the morning? The solution to create morning habits that boost productivity. The following habits can double your productivity and can be implemented immediately upon waking up.

1. Wake Up at 5 AM

Waking up early is a ritual that will double or triple your productivity. The time you miss out when you're waking up late or even normal morning hours can be assigned to doing your hardest task that relieve you of the stress for the rest of the day and "rewire" your brain for productivity in the morning. Most people wake up at 8 AM or 9 AM -

some even wake up at 10 AM or the afternoon. To become successful, you must wake up at least 2-3 hours before everyone else. Set your alarm clock to 5 AM or even 4 AM and start working early in the dawn. This routine will give you 2-3 hours ahead of everyone else to get the most important task of the day done.

Remember that the mind is the clearest within the first 3 morning hours upon waking up. If you use the hours before actual work hours, you can get the hardest task of your day done by the time everyone else wakes up. This gives you an edge over everyone else because you're utilizing excess hours to boost your productivity and you can assign those hours to fitness or other mind exercises such as meditation. If you're used to waking up late, this will be a daunting task for you to achieve but the body adjusts to a new habit in as little as 1-2 weeks. Waking up early won't work unless you go to bed early, so push your bed time backwards. If you go to bed at midnight and wake up at 7 AM, go to bed at 10 PM and wake up at 5 AM. This way you'll get your full night's rest and be able to start off in the early morning hours.

2. Drink a Bottle of Water

Water boosts energy to a higher degree than coffee. Most people don't realize the effects water has on energy levels in the body. We're all heard "hydration" keeps us healthy, but we never pay attention to the increase in energy high hydration produces. Our bodies were designed to consume water, and this is why we can go up to 40 days of no food if can still drink water. Without water? You'd only last a week.

Water is the most essential substance for the internal organs, and water can boost the energy levels of a person by a margin of 100%. If you wake up feeling energy less and you opt for coffee, accompany that with a bottle of water. The body is very slow in the morning because it's waking up from sleep, but when you put water into your body it's quickly assigned to the most necessary parts: the blood stream, the skin, the brain, the muscles.

Water accelerates blood flow by accelerating the bloodstream and this gives you an energizing feel. Staying hydrated also gives the skin a fresh look as opposed to a dry morning look. Water is even proven to increase sex drive in the morning by increasing the blood flow to our reproductive organs. The body adjusts to your individual consumption of water: If you drink one large bottle in the morning, you will likely have to go to the bathroom multiple times that day. However, once your body gets acclimated to consuming 3 or 4 large bottles a day, you will feel almost no inclination to flush the water out. Water consumption is a habit, one that invigorates your skin, gives you energy and supplies your internal organs with the nourishment they require.

3. Limit Time on Emails

Admit it: the first thing you did upon waking up is to check your phone for notifications and emails. If you're working in corporate America, your inbox is likely full every day. If you miss one day of emails, you may fall behind on your schedule. This makes you paranoid because you check our emails multiple times a day. Emails are productivity killers because they distract us from our main task of the morning. The emails in the morning make us think we have 20 different tasks to accomplish, but deep down we know which task of the day is the most important that would push us forward. This is why you should limit the time you spend on your emails and only check your inbox once, then go to work immediately.

If you spend more time on your emails, you'll focus on tasks you're supposed to do in the future which will further distract you from your daily goals. Give your emails one glance in the morning to make sure nothing's on fire. If things look casual, don't look at your emails until the evening and focus on work.

4. Don't Eat Breakfast

Contrary to popular belief, breakfast is not the most important meal of the day. In fact, breakfast is the biggest productivity killer for most people throughout the day. Replace your breakfast with a cup of coffee or a bottle of water to allow your body to "activate" internal organs by supplying it with essential hydration. This way the body can activate internally and flush out and debris that was accumulated from your food consumption the day before.

If you start your day by consuming food, you will load your body on items it doesn't need and lower your energy levels because you opted for food instead of water. Almost all breakfast options in the modern world contain high-carbs: bread, pancakes, cereal, bagels, and other variations of heavy breakfasts. This temporarily fills people but then their energy dips mid-day. If you want to kill your energy on purpose, start by eating a heavy breakfast in the morning. By mid-afternoon, you'll start "feeling sleepy" and you'll want to nap on your work day.

Pro Tip: When you feel like sleeping mid-day, this is your nutrition at work. The breakfast you consumed is slowly killing your internal energy and halving your sugar levels. This is why you feel a desire to sleep.

To avoid a steep decline in energy, skip breakfast and replace your breakfast with a large bottle of water and a cup of coffee. This will give you equal energy as consuming breakfast, but your energy levels won't dip mid-day. You also won't feel that fat-belly feeling but your stomach, but it will empty out and prepare you for lunch when you can consume high-nutrition foods. If you absolutely have to eat in the morning, go for a light breakfast such as a banana, apple or some eggs. Avoid all forms of pastry and sugary foods, as those are the biggest energy killers in the morning.

5. Do the Largest Task in the First 3 Hours

When you wake up, you'll know which task you must do that will require the most energy and effort - this is your "main task" of the day. This is the biggest productivity tip for people who struggle getting things done: Get that task done first, and everything else will seem like a breeze. Start working on your main task the minute you wake up. This way, your brain will get the proof it needs that the hardest task is under control, and you'll get it done in a few hours. Try to complete the task within 2-3 hours because those hours are your most prolific in the morning. The first hour upon waking up is the easiest to focus on tasks because your brain has peak mental clarity, and it progressively diminishes over the day. Start your day by doing the hardest task of the day.

Most people start by doing light tasks that don't require a lot of effort. This is a big mistake because they do a sloppy job on the first tasks and then once they "gather the courage" to do the big task they've already ran out of mental energy. The right way to stay on top of your productivity is to wake up and immediately treat work as if you're going to war: Start with the hardest project, then once you've got that off your back focus on smaller, less important projects.

6. Put a Clock in Front of You

If you're struggling starting things and you take a very long time to start a project, put a clock on your desk. Place a clock in the lower-right side of your computer, a clock on your phone or a physical clock — any clock will do. If you're reminded of the time often, you will become aware of how fast it passes and this will inject a "sense of urgency" in you that will prompt you to get things done faster. Placing a clock in front will also allow you to measure how long you take to complete tasks. This way, you can optimize your work to complete tasks faster.

Example: If you work at a call center and you call clients to pitch over the phone, you might find that you're only calling 5 people an hour. If you have a clock near you, this will tempt you to call more and you will end up making more calls and closing more. The more you're aware of time, the more you become aware of how you spend your work day. Developing a sense of urgency will give you the leverage you need to become less hesitant and take more action at work.

4 Evening Routines to End the Day Just Right

You've had a successful day — you completed all your big tasks, you closed new deals, you traveled back and forth to work. What will you do in the evening? The evening is a time to unwind and a time to prepare for the next day to make it successful. The evening is critical for the routines you set in place and forming new habits. This time of the day doesn't have to be a time for relaxation! Instead of lying in bed and watching TV in the evening, you can optimize those hours for exercise and this will improve your fitness which ultimately improves your energy levels throughout the day and making you more productive.

Night hours are ideal for re-shaping your body and mind because you're almost drained of energy, and you the little energy you have left can be assigned to activities that make an impact in your physical and mental shape. What are the best evening routines? Should you meditate, hit the gym, do yoga, prepare for work tomorrow — or do all those at once? The answer is that it depends on your situation. If you're lacking in physical activity, assign all your evening hours to fitness-related activities. If you're lacking in productivity, assign your evening hours to increasing productivity. The following are the best all-around evening routines that will help you complete your day and prepare you for another day of productivity.

1. Set up an Exercise Routine

Exercise is for the evenings, not the mornings. If you believe that you gain energy from exercise, ask yourself: Have you really exercised if you feel MORE energetic after the exercise than before? Exercising is all about draining yourself — you feel a surplus of energy and you release that energy by running, lifting weights and doing exercises that push you to your limits. Exercise stimulates endorphins, boosts blood flow and makes you look great. If you only exercise for 30 days and you've never exercised before, there's a chance you'll look very different. Your jaw will become more chiseled and defined, you'll start losing fat, and you'll feel high energy throughout the day.

If you exercise in the mornings, you'll only kill your energy because the energy that you use for productivity will diminish as it went into your morning exercise. However, if you exercise at night, you will experience the following: 1) You will be able to go "all out" because you don't have to spare any energy 2) You will tire yourself out and fall asleep more easily. If you struggle to fall asleep at night, setting up an exercise routine will tire you out and make you sleep like a baby. If you have high energy all throughout the day, it's logical to end your day by draining yourself of that energy through heavy exercise. The ideal time to exercise is 1-2 hours before you go to bed. If your bed time is at 10 PM, start exercising at 8-9 PM. This way you'll have enough time to carry out your exercise routine, shower, and prepare for bed.

Daily Self-Discipline

The best night exercises for you are ones that cater to your current abilities and goals. If you want to lose weight fast, you should opt for HIIT — high intensity interval training. This is a method of sprinting at 90-100% capacity by running as fast as possible. The average training routine consists of 10-20 of these sprints with little breaks in-between until you run out of energy.

If you choose a less intense workout, you should aim to start jogging long-distance. Start by doing short 10-minute jogs and then progressively increase your distance every week. If you feel that you're about to faint and you're losing energy - stop. Don't over-stretch yourself on the first few exercises only because you're feeling motivated. Take your time to progressively increase your exercises.

If you want to gain weight, you should consider getting a gym membership for access to heavy equipment. The average gym is stacked with thousands of dollars' worth of technology that is inaccessible to home-gym owners. The fitter you become, the higher your energy levels will be in the office. This in turn will reflect in your productivity because you'll be able to focus for longer hours, your output quality will increase and you will tire less. Fitness also makes us less responsive to heavy weather — if you're feeling cold in the winter months, you'll feel less cold when you're fit. The opposite applies for hot weather - fit people are usually not bothered by extreme heat.

Pro Tip: Stop relying on fitness apps to track your progress. If you rely on technology you will lose touch with your body's nature: you'll think in terms of miles, hours and calories. Forget that! Start exercising and push yourself without technology and you will eventually become familiar with your physical abilities. You will instinctively know how much you can run and push yourself progressively.

Daily Self-Discipline

2. Meditate for 20 Minutes

Do you feel unable to focus because you're distracted by everything and even when you start, you can't seem to keep your attention on one task for long? The solution is to get out of your head! We're naturally consumed by our thoughts and this gets distracting because while we're supposed to be working, we daydream about events that have no correlation to our work. How do we get out of our own head? The only way to be effective is to become present. If you have no thoughts and you immerse ourselves in the present moment, you can become more productive, more engaged with your work and produce higher-quality output. The practice that teaches the art of presence is meditation. Anyone can start meditating at home for free.

Pro Tip: You only need to assign 15-20 minutes at night to perfect your meditation. You don't have to meditate like a Buddhist Monk 12 hours a day to be successful in meditation.

The art of meditation can be summed up as "not thinking." Being present is about immersing yourself with the present moment. Imagine yourself playing basketball — you focus on shooting the hoops, you enjoy passing the ball, you anticipate fellow players passing you the ball, you're completely immersed with the game. This is what's known as "becoming present."

Do you even feel in the zone when you're out on a Friday night, you're drinking with your buddies and the conversation keeps flowing? This is also being present. People consume alcohol because it allows them to get out of their head and become present. However, the practice can be replicated naturally by teaching yourself to get out of your own way. It's easier than you think: Start by sitting on the floor of your room, preferably somewhere where you won't be distracted by noises and other people. Then, you can engage in your first mediation session.

How it works: Set an alarm clock for 15 or 20 minutes, depending on how long you think you'll last with your eyes closed. Clasp your hands together and close your eyes. Now focus on your breath and stop thinking — don't even think about not thinking, only focus your attention on the breath. Eventually, you'll start feeling a deep relaxation effect. This usually happens once you're 5 minutes in the session. You'll eventually be fully immersed in the present moment, and then the clock will ring. You'll open your eyes slowly, the world will seem like it's surreal and moving slow. This is how you know you've achieved a fully present meditation session. Once you've practiced meditation consistently for a month, you'll naturally evoke your present feeling and you'll become more confident because you'll be stuck in head way less. There are also joint meditation areas and places where you can practice meditation with other people.

3. Take a Cold Shower

Cold showers are the most extreme, but they're for people who want to push their endurance to the maximum and get in touch with their nature. Cold showers can make you stronger, more in touch with your primal nature, push your endurance and experience health benefits. Think about the old days: Humanity has evolved for millions of years and we've only had hot showers for the last hundred years. Yet, we think that hot showers are the default and cold showers are "extreme." The cold shower is how we used to shower for most of humanity's history, and this is why the practice carries numerous benefits.

The main benefits of cold showers are a rush of dopamine, stimulation of fat-burning and an increase blood flow. However, in practice cold showers have certain "invisible" benefits that manifest themselves over the long term. Cold showers shock your system and supply your nervous system with a "wake up call" similar to that of coffee in the morning. The initial shock makes the nervous system crave radical substances less, and it can help you quit chemical addictions such as cigarettes or drugs. Cold showers completely replace the need your body has for external stimulation.

One more major benefit to cold showers is that you don't feel cold in winter, as cold showers make you resilient to cold and you barely feel anything when you're out in the coldest winter months. Certain communities in Russia practice jumping in ice because cold hits their nervous system to the degree that they feel immune to cold in daily life.

Taking a cold shower should be done progressively. You can't just jump in freezing cold water without pacing yourself first. However, you also shouldn't call a shower a "cold shower" if you shower with hot water and only release 5-10 seconds of cold at the end. A cold shower has to last at least 3-5 minutes to be successful. Start by watering your legs and slowly feeling the cold water hitting your skin. You'll feel shivers all over your body because your body is experiencing the cold water. Then spread some cold water among the upper parts of your body and get used to the temperature. After you've acclimated to the cold for a minute or two, you can get under a full shower blast for a couple of seconds. This will be very shocking to you, but if you embrace it you will eventually get used to it.

Pro Tip: Imagine a cold shower like jumping in a lake. The lake has colder water than an ocean, but once you're inside for 2-3 minutes – the water doesn't feel as cold. The same applies to cold showers. Slow step them and picture yourself as if you're in a lake. You'll eventually learn to handle low temperatures.

4. Read a Book Chapter (Offline)

Go to your favorite book store and pick up a book that will help you in real life. This can be a book related to fitness, business, your profession, or anything that relates to your personal growth. Get the paperback version and get off the internet. This way you can fully engage with the book. If the book is not too large, aim to read a full chapter per day. By consuming the right information, you will improve your life and it will add a sense of "completion" once you've read a full chapter each night. This will also help you fall asleep naturally, if you struggle to get a full night's rest. It's better to read paperback editions because most tablets and laptops have light beaming into your eyes. This is harmful, especially if you're reading at night with the lights out.

Eat These 3 Foods for a Productive Brain

Does your head feel foggy and drowsy after you eat breakfast? Do you feel tired in the afternoon and want to pass out on your office chair? Do you find it hard to get out of bed, to work long hours, to exercise or do anything remotely challenging? This is not due to a lack of motivation — this is caused by your brain reacting to nutrition. The brain consumes 20% of all nutrition (calories) that enter the body, which means that the quality of your food directly reflects in the quality of your brain functioning. If you ever wondered why "organic" food is more expensive and mass-produced food cheap, the difference is due to the quality of the nutrients.

Nutrition is not about how shiny your 6-pack abs are: It's about the clarity of your mental state, the consistency of your focus, and the productivity output you leave at the end of each day. Those are all controlled by one single thing: your food intake. If you put the right foods in your body, your brain will register and function at a higher level. It will allow you to work harder, provide longer focus and enable you to do the tasks that you find challenging.

If you eat the right foods, you'll be able to perform at superhuman levels. You'll work 10-hour shifts easily, you'll run more miles without exhausting yourself, you'll think clearly and become more confident. People report that their "brain fog" disappears once they started consuming the right food. There are many foods that affect the brain positively, but the ones listed below make the biggest difference. If you want to immediately boost your performance, to feel higher energy and long-lasting focus — focus on the foods below.

1) Greens: Broccoli, Spinach, Kale

The three kings of green (broccoli, spinach and kale) are the most essential brain foods that make a night and day difference in the way your brain performs. If you had to eat only 3 foods for the rest of your life choose the top 3 greens: broccoli, spinach and kale. These 3 foods alone are better than almost every other food for removing brain fog and establishing mental clarity. Broccoli is arguably the most nutrient-rich food in the world - it contains all the right Omega-3 fatty acids that build and repair brain cells in the fraction of a millisecond, and it even has anti-aging and weight-loss properties. Broccoli's effects on the brain can be felt immediately! Once you consume a full head of broccoli, you'll feel as if a horse kicked you in the head. The effects are so powerful and they clear your brain that no other food comes close.

Pro Tip: Take 2 days to experiment the effects of food on your brain. The first day, consume the greasiest food you can find: Hamburgers, pizza, pasta. The second day, eat broccoli and spinach and mix them together. Observe the effects on your brain and your energy levels 2 hours after you consume each. You'll notice a significant upgrade in mental clarity once you consume broccoli vs. a low-energy drowsy feeling once you consume greasy food. This is why the latter cost more — they are higher quality.

The following happens when you consume greens: You start waking up, your brain starts oozing energy and you achieve maximum brain clarity. This is the effect of high nutrients penetrating your brain and supplying it with the nourishment it needs. Greens are consumed by athletes because they boost strength and endurance on the field. As a result, you can run longer and lift heavier weights if your mental state is clear. Broccoli, spinach and kale have almost identical effects and these are all premium and expensive foods. Ideally you should consume green foods at least once a day. Learn to appreciate the subtle, little flavors in greens if you currently have problems with the taste. If you can't find them due to seasoning, most supermarkets have frozen variations. You can cook them a million different ways and mix them with tasty spices.

2. Nuts and seeds

Nuts are the most nutrient-dense foods for the brain after greens. They are loaded with positive ingredients that enhance our cognitive functions. The most notable in the "nuts" category are cashews and almonds, which provide the highest stimulation for the brain and they are the perfect snack food for uplifting energy and keeping us sharp and focused. Nuts can't be consumed as a main course, but they are very effective as side-foods that which be consumed alongside main meals. Nuts such as cashews and almonds provide the highest density of fats and proteins that serve as the building block for brain muscle.

To strengthen your brain muscles, you should regularly consume nuts. Cashews and almonds are also filled with omega-3 acids and antioxidants that enhance mental clarity. Scientific studies link cashews to improved cognitive function with older age and studies discovered that they can offset old-age diseases such as Alzheimer's which are linked to the cognitive ability. They can work wonders for healthy, young individuals. Make sure not to go overboard on nuts because they are very calorie-dense and they can be fattening if consumed in copious amounts. A handful of nuts is enough for a day.

3. Fish

Fish and fish oil is essential for cognitive ability because fish contains the highest density of Omega-3 acids. Omega-3's are essential repair blocks that the brain uses to formulate brain cells and increase blood flow in the brain area. Fish have the highest density of Omega-3's, making them essential for cognitive ability and productivity. Oily fish take the lead in terms of omega-3 rich fish, in particular canned tuna. Do you ever open a can of tuna and think the oil is bad for you? It's actually oil that your brain craves — it's linked to better cognitive abilities, increase in thinking skill and brain clarity.

Salmon is also an exceptional brain food, albeit a bit more expensive. To boost your brain function, make fish part of your weekly food consumption. You might want to take it a step further and learn how to cook fish instead of relying on canned tuna. Pick up some frozen fish from your supermarket, lay it down in some oil and let it cook for 30-40 minutes. Combine it with tasty lemons or mix it with greens, and enjoy the optimal lunch for brain power.

BONUS: 4. Coffee

Coffee deserves an honorable mention among the top brain ingredients that boosts concentration, productivity and improves our mood. Do you look forward to your morning only for the coffee? Coffee is an acquired taste because it has a bitter flavor, but once a person gets used to the taste, they learn to appreciate coffee and look forward to the bitterness. You feel "alert" when you drink coffee because caffeine has an active ingredient that blocks the brain's chemicals known as "adenosines."

Adenosine chemicals can be released in the morning and during the day as well. This is why coffee is imperative in keeping us alert and productive. One cup of coffee can supply you with an energy boost that lasts until mid-day when you have your lunch. Make sure not to go overboard on coffee — 2 cups a day is enough. Sip a cup of coffee once you've woken up, and delay the second cup until you've accomplished your work tasks and you feel ready to "reward" yourself.

15 Daily Affirmations to Teach Your Brain Self-Discipline

Affirmations are essentially self-talk that we communicate to our subconscious mind in order to demand the willpower we require to achieve our goals. The brain recognizes affirmations as crossing the border between "I want to do something" to "I will do something" — taking concrete action. Affirmations play a significant role in our transformation when set high goals because they can affect our self-belief system and incentivize us to take action. Affirmations can be applied to all areas of life. They are simple statements that you repeat to yourself when you wake up and when you go to bed.

The way to base affirmations is to consider your personal goals (not everyone can apply the same affirmations). One can create affirmations for losing weight, one can create business affirmations, one can create affirmations related to self-confidence. To determine an area where you need affirmations, think about your biggest problem in the moment. Ask yourself: What am I struggling with? Where could I improve in life? The answer to those questions is what you should base your affirmations on.

The #1 Rule of Affirmations

The base rule of affirmations is that affirmations must be positive. An affirmation cannot be negative because the subconscious mind does not recognize negative affirmations — it only recognizes positive affirmations.

✗**Negative affirmation**: I won't delay my workout anymore.

✓**Positive affirmation**: I will start working out tonight.

Affirmations must be positive, and they must be written in the first person. You must always use "I" when you write an affirmation. This registers in your brain as you referring to yourself, and it rewires your psychology for new habits. The ideal amount of affirmations per goal is between 5 or 10 affirmations. Write your affirmations down on a piece of paper and read them in the morning and before you go to sleep. You can come up with 5 affirmations for every goal. Here are some examples of affirmations based on different goals.

Example: 5 Affirmations for Weight Loss

1. I will improve my food habits and eat healthy food.

2. I will drink 3 bottles of water per day.

3. I will exercise every night.

4. I will run sprints every night at 9 PM.

5. I will get a gym membership.

Example: 5 Affirmations for Work

Daily Self-Discipline

1. I will wake up at 5 AM every morning.

2. I will start working immediately.

3. I will do the hardest task first thing in the morning.

4. I will focus on my work completely.

5. I will work every day without taking days off.

Example: 5 Affirmations for Dating

1. I will get in shape to become more attractive.

2. I will buy better clothes to make a better impression.

3. I will start going out every weekend.

4. I will meet new people and go on dates.

5. I will find my ideal partner.

Rule #2: Must Be About the Present

The affirmations you write must relate to the present moment. You must focus your affirmations on daily actions that you can take as early as tomorrow. If an affirmation is out of your reach or too into the future, discard it. Only focus on affirmations that you relate to your present struggles.

Ask yourself: What can you do now? The answer: You can wake up early, you can eat better, you can exercise, you can meet new people. What can't you do now? You can't start a business overnight. Affirmations exist to help us after we've navigated through our goals and we know the big-picture of where we're headed; affirmations effectively re-shape our mind in order to focus on immediately achievable goals and "push" us towards taking action.

Chapter 6 - Tools for Future Success

5 Exercises to Test and Maintain Powerful Self-Discipline

Do you feel overwhelmed by big tasks that require a lot of willpower? Would you rather start small by accomplishing small tasks that give you the confidence and willpower to move on to large tasks? Willpower has to be built gradually like a muscle. If you have no weight training experience and immediately start benching 100 pounds at the gym, you will put strain on your muscles. Meanwhile benching 100 pounds bars is a piece of cake for someone who's practiced with 20 pounds bars, 50 pounds bars and 100 pounds bars progressively. Why don't you practice progressively too? To work your way up to the highest willpower goals, you must start with small goals and then once you've gained the confidence, attempt to take a swing the big ones.

Warning: **You must start now.** If you delay your big goals endlessly, time will eventually catch up with you and you'll regret not taking action now. Do you look back at things you wanted to do 5 years ago and wish you got started back then for all the years wasted? Now is the best time to start. Let's start by doing some small exercises that you can accomplish on your own. If you do the exercises here, you'll build a baseline for future willpower. You can also create your own exercises: ones that cater to your individual goals.

Pro Tip: Small exercises help set the baseline for willpower. Even a tiny exercise such as washing the dishes can increase your willpower. When we're out of willpower, we feel like doing nothing. Once we shift in gear, our willpower muscle starts growing and we gradually progress onto bigger tasks.

Treat Exercises as Monthly Challenges

Treat the following exercises the way you do challenges: Do you remember popular challenges such as the 30-day no-shave challenge? Each one of these exercises can be repeated on a daily basis and you can form your own challenges to retain the habits. Example: Create a "30-day no-TV challenge" where you challenge yourself to stop watching TV at night once you're back from work and you instead spend your time meditating or reading a book for 30 days.

Exercise #1: No-Sugar Coffee

The first challenge relates to something we all consume in the morning — coffee. You essentially have to drink bitter, sugarless coffee for 30 days. What will you accomplish? It will push you to get out of your comfort taste for 30 days. The sugar added sweetness to your coffee, but now you'll taste real coffee. Train your brain to enjoy the subtle flavors in bitter coffee and consume it slowly. This will teach you that taste is acquired. Eventually you can improve your nutrition by consuming foods that you didn't find tasty, only for their brain benefits such as broccoli and spinach.

Exercise #2: No Social Media

Deactivate your social media for 30 days. This one is tough if you have an extroverted personality. Your Facebook account? Delete it. Your Instagram? Gone. Your dating apps? Discard them all. Spend 30 days interacting with people in real life and only use your phone to make calls. Remove the pings that you get from the notifications panel during the day. What will this accomplish? It will remove your need to check your phone impulsively waiting on your next dopamine hit.

This way you can effectively focus on your work and all your attention will shift to producing better output instead of watching what your buddy Brad streaming his fishing trip in Canada.

Exercise #3: Run Every Day Challenge

Let's say you exhaust yourself every night for 30 days. What will the results be? You could possibly lose between 20 pounds and 60 pounds, depending on how extreme your diet is. Contrary to popular belief, exercise does not impact weight loss as much as dieting and water consumption. The upside of exercise is the physical condition you build up.

Once your 30 days are up, this is what will happen: You will feel more powerful, you will feel increased energy in the morning, you will be able to concentrate more, and you'll refuse to stay locked inside your home at night. This 30-day exercise will build your willpower because right now you're tired and you don't feel like doing anything. In 30 days, you'll naturally crave exercise every day. Remember: It's all about the consistency. You don't have to run every night, but you must come out for the routine – take a walk instead. The part that matters is that you're consistent.

Exercise #4: Clean Your Apartment Every Week

Take one day every week to reevaluate the items in your apartment and consider everything you own. Are those items essential to your productivity or are they hindering it? Is the state of your apartment preventing you from working, exercising, meditating or cooking healthy foods that help you? Stand in the middle of your apartment and look around: Observe everything. Do you really need that Buddhist statue you brought home from your Cambodia trip? Do you really need all those clothes from 5 years ago?

Is there too much clutter in your kitchen? Do you have too many heavy snacks and food that zaps your energy? Put them in the trash. Donate your old clothes to the Red Cross. Sell the electronics and toys. Leave only the things that are necessary for productivity — your essentials such as clothes, laptops and weights. Repeat the same for your desktop computer. Too many times we have distracting icons such as games, movies and other distractions that have no relation to our work. Remove them all. Do a clean-up every week.

Exercise #5: Meditate Every Night

Start meditating every night for 30 nights in a row. You can learn meditation in as little as 5 sit-downs, but 30 meditation nights in a row will make you a master in the practice. Meditation is about invoking the present moment and getting in touch with presence. When you meditate you feel completely at peace and you get out of your head. You think less, and you observe things as they are, not as you process them through your ego. Once you've grown accustomed to the practice, repeat it often until you can naturally invoke the feeling. If you feel that you need to delay your meditation, that's when you need it the most. Remember to take at least 20 minutes a night for the practice and cut off all distractions while you do it.

How to Create Lasting Self-Awareness

If someone told you "Go run 10 miles now" – what would you do? If you were pushed under a cold shower for 5 minutes – would you run out of the shower? Are you fully aware of your capabilities on the mental and physical level? Self-awareness is the act of discovering who you are — your own physical and mental capabilities and limits. We all have a surface-level self-awareness and know what can do approximately. However, you need to practice if you wish to develop high self-awareness and know exactly what you're capable of no matter the task.

We must test our abilities constantly to become fully aware of what we can do and can't do. Let's say you think you can run 10 miles without stopping. When is the last time you attempted to run 10 miles? What if you ran for 5 miles and you gasped for air and couldn't do it? You can't tell until you try — you need to try it out. Once you know what you can do, you can progressively increase your limits. This practice applies to all matters of life! To elevate beyond basic self-awareness, you must push yourself constantly and test your own behavior. There are practices that can help you discover lasting self-awareness.

Self-Awareness Is for Action-Takers

Self-awareness is about knowing what you can do and what you can't do by testing this on the field. This reinforces your ego in a good way because you've already tested what you can accomplish and you feel prepared to tackle your big goals. There is another underlying layer to self-awareness: How your behaviors impact people around you. Once you recognize how your behaviors and productivity are impacting people, you can adjust your output to create more of that desired feeling.

Example: If you're a musician, you can improve people's lives because your music makes them feel better. Once you recognize the kind of songs that impact people in the best way, you can create more songs that emulate that. This is because you've become self-aware. The practice applies in business: Once you learn what your clients like by testing it, you can deliver more of that product. Effectively self-awareness translates to all areas of life. It reveals how we perceive ourselves and how others perceive us.

You can't develop self-awareness by staying at home, so you must go out into the real world and discover who you are by continually taking action. The following practices will help you obtain a high level of self-awareness:

1. Travel to Foreign Countries

Travel to a country as opposite of your culture as possible: as long as the destination is safe, go take a few weeks off and book a hotel. Pack your bags, book the flights, get your visa stamps - go out into the world. When you get to a foreign culture, you will be tested on all levels: Your social skills when you try to communicate with people who barely speak English, your street knowledge when you end up in shady areas by accident and even the general perception of who you are. Foreign people who have no relation to you and see you for the first time will tell you their honest impressions of you. They'll try to guess where you're from, make conversation about your country/accent/fashion and this will let you know how people who are completely foreign perceive you.

In essence, you will develop a deep knowledge of your identity, your origins, the way you live life and how others perceive you. Travel will boost your self-awareness tenfold. You don't have to interact with people who are completely distant to your culture. In fact, any environment that you're not used to will suffice. The way you navigate when you get lost in a foreign country, the way you experience new cultures and the way you interact with people will reinforce your identity to the highest level. If you're still trying to "find yourself," travel is the best way to achieve that. Travel is cheap, as even intercontinental flights are now inexpensive.

2. Engage in Flow-State Activities

Daily Self-Discipline

Why do you do some things effortlessly while you have to coax yourself into doing work? Compare how little effort it takes you to play a game vs. do a hard task at work. When you play a video game, you don't have to prepare yourself — you know it's easy and go get into the game easily. When you try to do work it's hard and overwhelming, this is why it takes patience for you to engage with that task. In both cases, you enter what's called a "flow state." The difference is that you get in a flow state with a game immediately while at work it takes longer. Imagine you're skiing down a hill. Your speed accelerates as you fly down the snow, and you can't seem to stop. This is what being in a flow state is all about.

The ideal flow-state activity is one that is hard enough to require preparation, but not hard enough that it overwhelms you: think "medium difficulty." Example: Easy difficulty flow states are flow states that you get in instantly — watching movies, playing games, cooking — those require no effort. Hard difficulty flow states are ones that require massive preparation such as launching a new product in front of a crowd or similar life-changing events. What you need are medium-difficulty flow states: Working on a project, jogging at night, sitting down for a meditation session. These "flow state" activities are perfect self-awareness boosters, because they challenge you to get out of your comfort zone continually. This builds up over time and boosts your self-awareness in terms of what you're capable of doing.

3. Do Hard Tasks Every Day

Push yourself to do things you don't want to do on a daily basis — this will maximize yourself awareness. You'll know exactly what you can do, instead of guessing what you can do. Observe your body and what it responds to. Example: You want to eat, sleep, drink coffee, socialize. What don't you want to do? You don't want to work, you don't want to exercise, you don't want to wash the dishes. These are things you should do! The more you engage with tasks you don't want to do, the highest your willpower grows. Listen to your body and do the things you don't want to do.

If you focus on doing things you don't want to do, your brain will start to develop an inclination to do these without resistance. The initial resistance you're feeling when you start doing challenging tasks is a protection mechanism from overwhelming yourself. In order to push through the initial resistance, you must assign all your energy to the tasks that generate the resistance. This way, you will proactively break through your resistance and you will become a lot more competent in your field of work. Do harder tasks progressively – eventually doing hard things will become natural for you.

3 Healthy Habits for Better Concentration

Do you have this "one" task that you know could change your life, but you end up doing the opposite of the task? Do you think about 30 unrelated things when you know you should be focused on the task at hand? Are you easily distracted and is your environment enabling you to get away without working? Lack of concentration is the biggest productivity killer and you must address this to increase your productivity and move your life in the right direction. Concentration is a flow-state activity that requires patience — it can't be achieved instantly.

To be successful in concentration, you must slowly baby-step your way into the work process. We're falsely led to believe that concentrating is about us sitting down and completing our tasks Rambo-style until the whole work day is done. The truth is that the smallest things can impact our concentration: the environment, psychology, nutrition and even our goals (or lack thereof). If we have all those aligned, we can concentrate on a single task. If one of those is missing, we'll fall in the trap and fail to concentrate. We must start by cleaning our environment of items that influence our focus, and then progressively increase our work load until we achieve maximum concentration on any given task. The following habits help you concentrate on a daily basis.

1. Hand-pick Your Influences

Turn around and look at your office: What surrounds you? Are your colleagues productive or are they slacking on social media? Are there too many distractions nearby? What about your nutrition? What are you consuming? Cut off everything that doesn't help you: distractions, people, nutrition, non-work optimized environments – all of it. If you have a PlayStation/Xbox console and this is something you like to play, discard it in the trash. Let's say you have willpower to not play, should you still trash your console? Yes. The thought that you have it nearby will tempt you once you start working and need a break.

If you take cigarette breaks between work tasks, get rid of your cigarettes because they tempt you to think about work breaks. If your colleagues are not productive, stop talking to them. Concentration is not only about your personal output; it's also about the environment that surrounds you. If you live in an environment that is not optimized for productivity, you won't achieve anything. If you live in a productive environment that enables work, you will achieve a lot. Even minor influences such as snacks can affect your concentration. If you have snacks like chips on your desk, remove them because they increase your will to eat and make you less willing to work. Look at all the external influences that surround you and ask yourself if they're helping you or if they're distracting you from your purpose.

2. Disable the Internet

Disable the internet. This will cut off at least 50% of all your distractions. Unless the internet is absolutely imperative to your productivity (i.e. you trade stocks or sell online) completely cut it off during your work day. That's it — shut down the router and disable your phone too. The internet is the biggest concentration-killer because it gives us immediate access to everything. It's also the biggest instant-gratification tool humans have invented in history.

One distraction leads to another. Example: You start looking for medical equipment factories in Germany for your company. Suddenly you're looking up the town where they manufacture the medical equipment. You're then looking at flights to book to Germany and hotels. After that you notice some food in the hotel pictures and you want to try that food. The internet is a slippery slope as it creates one distraction that leads to another. Disable the router and re-enable it once you're done working. You will still have access to your computer, but you'll only focus on the task at hand. If you need the internet to do research for a project, complete the research for the project beforehand and then disable the internet while you do the actual work.

3. Increase Your Hard Tasks Progressively

To maximize concentration, you have to increase your flow-tasks progressively: Start with a hard task one day, and then once you're in the flow complete the easier tasks. The "hard" task will become "moderate" the next week. This way you can do harder and harder tasks by the week. You have to habituate yourself into concentration by tackling more difficult tasks every week. On the small scale, you must do hard tasks first because this will push you into a flow state of mind. On a large scale, you want to baby-step these hard tasks and take on heavier workloads progressively every week.

This applies to other areas of life such as fitness. If you start with 5-mile run, attempt a 10-mile run the next week because you'll have built up the condition. If you attempt a 10-mile run outright, you'll likely fail because you haven't progressed to that level. Increase your "hard" tasks progressively, and start with the most essential ones. Ask yourself: What would really change my life right now? If it's fitness, focus on fitness. If it's making money, focus on your job or a business. Increase the difficulty of your tasks and tackle them accordingly.

3 Unconventional Ways to Master Self-Discipline

Do you have a more "extreme" personality than the average person and wish to test out conventional ways to achieve your goals? Are you unsatisfied with the norm and do you push yourself way above the formalities and capacities of an average person? Some people are "wired" to outperform everyone else, that's why they opt for unconventional ways to increase their productivity and achieve their goals.

Warning: Certain unconventional ways are healthier than others. In theory, an "unconventional" way to increase productivity would be to consume prescription pills. The downside is that those are unhealthy and inconsistent, so your focus only runs as long as you take the pills. If you actually reinvent yourself and you create a new persona that can focus on the tasks, you'll be able to sustain your new habits forever. This guide focuses on unconventional ways that are both healthy and sustainable — ones that everyone can implement to reflect on their life and obtain high levels of self-discipline.

1. Audit Your Time Like the Tax-Man

What does Uncle Sam ask you at the end of each fiscal year? In essence the tax authorities inquire as to how you made your money. Every

Daily Self-Discipline

April 15th us as Americans have to provide records of salaries we received, bonuses, how we spent our money, what banking institutions we used, etc. The government holds us accountable for every dollar in our bank accounts they want to know the source of our income.

What if the government audited how you spent your day? Would you know where each minute went and how you choose to spend it? What if someone analyzed your average work day? This technique alone could double or triple your productivity. If you "audit" your time the way the government audits your bank account, you will be able to identify where your time leaks and determine where you can increase your output, allowing you to patch up time leaks and optimize your time for productivity.

Put a webcam in your office and record yourself for a day. What would you find out? Were you working the whole day or did you spend half of the time browsing the internet, eating, talking to coworkers and doing nothing? If you're record every minute of your day, you'll shocked at the time you end up wasting doing unproductive things. You may spend 6 hours not working and 2 hours actually working. Most people barely spend 1/3 of their work day actually working.

To increase the quality of your output, to produce more and to waste less time, you should start by auditing your time. Keep records of every hour to see what you've accomplished and how long your breaks lasted. You only have to do this for one day. Call it an "Audit Day" and review how your day went. Once you become aware as to the way your time leaks, you can put that time to use the next day. If you spent half of the time slacking off in different ways, use that time to double your productivity.

2. Picture Your Success

Daily Self-Discipline

What if you were assigned to become the CEO of a multimillion-dollar enterprise? What if you were the most successful doctor/lawyer/accountant in your state? What would your average day look like then? It certainly wouldn't look the same as your average day now. Think about what would happen if you were put in a high position in your field of work overnight. Now imagine what an average day would look like for you in that position. Would you be required to do more tasks, to wake up earlier, to create bigger projects? What would an average day look like for you?

Once you figure that out, write down the average day of successful you and repeat the steps as if you're successful now. Optimize your current average day to emulate the average day of your successful version. Once you replicate it, you will eventually obtain the same results they have. This is the act of "reverse-engineering" success. It's possible to tell how a person became successful by analyzing their work history and business moves. Everyone starts somewhere, but the difference is where we all end up. What did successful people in your field do to obtain their success? What did they do in the last 10 years? Did they make certain moves that you are too afraid to make? There was always something that pushed them to go beyond the average in their industry. Imagine yourself at the peak of your success and ask yourself: What did it take for you to get there? Repeat that.

3. Force Yourself to Work

When all other options fail, force yourself to do the things you don't want to do! Force is a harsh word, but in many cases it's necessary. Write down the things that you must do to be successful and gradually force yourself into the action-steps that would get you there. Example: Force yourself to wake up at 5 AM. Set the loudest alarm clock possible for 5 AM or set 2 alarm clocks that go off simultaneously. Once you hear the sounds, you will be forced to get out of bed. Every activity that you must do can be forced. Once you force yourself to do it once, your brain will receive the "proof" it needs that this is something you can do and it will become monumentally easier for you to repeat that the next day. If you can't make yourself do things the easy way, force yourself to do them the hard way.

3 Transformative Ways to Push Yourself to the Next Level

Do you feel that you're on the brink of doing something excellent? Are you feeling deep motivation and you can tell you're on the brink of changing your whole life? Maybe you need that slight little "push" that will allow you to go over the edge and make the first move towards a better life. This is how you know you're ready to elevate yourself!

So you're feeling motivated, you have your goals and to-do's written down and you're excited to get started. All you need are a few more tips that give you a better perspective as to how you should go about taking action. These transformative techniques are for the action-taker — the person who acts on their dreams daily and don't dwell too much planning. If you're ready to jump in, start by applying the following transformative techniques:

1. Be Ready, Not Prepared

If you prepare forever, you will never become prepared enough! You will always hold off until you do one imaginary obstacle, then invent another obstacle. Imagine you're ready right now and start doing the things you want right now. Let's say you want to start a restaurant but you're 10 months away from saving the money you need to open a location. Why wait the 10 months? Start by producing the dishes you will have in your restaurant today. Write down creative names for the dishes, create a menu with prices like you'd have in your restaurant and invite your friends for an "experiment" where they act as the customers and you serve them in your restaurant.

If you're trying to get in shape, why wait 3 months or 6 months from now? Even if you're loaded on work, you'll still have 1-2 hours at the end of each night that you can assign to exercise. Addictions are the worst! If you hold off the "quit date" on your addiction, you might find yourself holding it off forever. Switch your mindset from "waiting to be prepared" to "I'm ready right now." You can force yourself to be ready and remove your imaginary obstacles - start now.

2. Aim to Do More, Faster

If you have a task that requires you to do in 10 days, try to do it in 5. Let's say you have a big business pitch to make and it takes you 10 days to do the research, gather the slides, present the products and make the presentation. What if suddenly the deadline was shifted to 5 days? Would you be able to do it? Chances are, you would. Now even if the deadline is not moved and you have 10 days, act as if you have 5 days! This will create a sense of urgency and you'll be able to get your projects done in half the time.

You will be shocked at the speed in which you can tackle your "big" projects once you shorten your deadlines. Most people delay their projects or wait until they only have a few days to the deadline in order to start taking action. If you allocate every day you're given to your work, you'll be able to get things done in half the time. If it takes you 15 minutes to run the track, aim to do it in 7 minutes next time. The less time you have, the more inclined you will be to take action. Even if you have unlimited time, create artificial deadlines and make yourself achieve the tasks within those deadlines.

3. Use the Gun-to-the-Head Technique

Imagine a terrorist came and put a gun to your head and told you, "Get that task done today or I pull the trigger." What would you do? Would you delay your task and browse the internet while you casually talk to your colleagues? Or would you diligently spend every minute working on the project? The "Gun-to-the-Head" technique is to imagine that your life is in danger and that unless you do the task you're going to die. Once our body activates our survival instinct, we go above and beyond to do things that we otherwise deemed impossible.

Imagine someone put a gun to your head and told you to run 10 miles. You would run faster than an Olympic runner. However, if you had the comfort of staying inside and watching movies, running 10 miles would seem like an exhausting task for you. It's all about perspective. Once you run out of options and you're feeling unproductive, simply imagine someone put a gun to your temple and forced you to do what needs to be done. Remember the phrase: "When you have a why, you'll find a how.

Conclusion

This book is your wake-up call. It's the sign you've been waiting for!

You have the techniques. Now, it's high time to put them to use.

STOP HOLDING OUT!

This book sheds light on the biggest problems in daily motivation and self-discipline. To succeed, implement what resonated with you the most. Consume all the information. Try it out. Use this book as a reminder when you forget basic principles, to keep you on track and kick you in the butt when you start slipping.

Do you remember all those times when you told yourself, "I'll do it when I'm ready"? Now is the time — your "one day" has come! You know exactly what you need to do in order to achieve your dreams. If you've held off your purpose in life for an unknown date, if you've held back your energy and hoped for a better time — remember that there is no better time than the present moment to start.

If we leave you with anything, it's to have faith in yourself.

You will have many downturns along your journey. You will experience a lot of upsides too.

Discover who you are, discover where you're headed, and take action.

All humans are flawed, but the techniques here would help us live with our flaws. We hope you've developed a better understanding as to the mysterious ways human nature works and how our biology is wired to function against our interests. We hope you get to know who you are and grow self-awareness through trials and tribulations. Our evolutionary nature and our goals in modern society conflict with each other. To make our evolutionary nature and modern society work, we have to apply a set of techniques that combine the best sides of both.

Use resistance as your compass.

The friction we feel on our path is resistance — the most powerful force of nature. Resistance preserves the status quo: it's a protective mechanism that protects us from stepping into the unknown. Resistance prevents from changing thinking that it's in our best interest. To do anything different, we have to shock our system and push through resistance. Resistance serves as a compass to point us towards the things we should really be doing. If you feel unwilling to work on your goals, feel the resistance in your body. The resistance tells you exactly what to do. Resistance signals that you're preparing for something great, that something is right behind the corner. If you push through it, you will come out a completely different person on the other end. Deep down, you know what that "thing" is.

Don't delay your dreams — start now.

This book covered the most important methods and techniques to help you establish daily self-discipline. Now is the time to convert all you've learned into action.

As a last note, remember this fact: We're all different.

You have to create your own motivation, your own techniques, your own disciplines. You are your own person with your own goals, your own dreams and your own circumstances. You're not forced to implement every technique we teach, and it's not important to do them all at once. It's up to you to figure out what works for you and apply your own spins on the techniques, based on your own individual experiences of operating and goals in life.

Daily Self-Discipline

Start by doing something — anything. See where life takes you. Your journey in life is different to the journey of 7 billion other humans on the planet. Once you discover what works for you, start doing and aim for the stars.

Beat Procrastination and Get The Job Done

Do You Feel Like a Lazy Bear Watching the Days Go By? Get Thing Done by Breaking Bad Habits and Find Limitless Motivation, Even If you're Lazy AF

Table of Contents

INTRODUCTION	**127**
CHAPTER ONE: QUIT BAD HABITS NOW	**131**
The Biggest Misconceptions about Laziness	131
5 Reasons Why You Are Lazy And How To Fix Them	133
6 Ways to Overcome the Lazy Brain	137
7 Terrible Habits that Keep you from Success	140
CHAPTER TWO: FIRING UP A MOTIVATED MIND	**144**
Which Type of Procrastinator are you?	144
10 Must-Know Hacks for Mind-Blowing Motivation	151
The Fixed Mindset vs the Growth Mindset	155
5 Tips for Developing a Mindset That Brings You Success	157
CHAPTER THREE: GETTING THE JOB DONE	**160**
11 Essential Techniques to Power Up Your Productivity	160
10 Secrets Behind Productivity According to the World's Billionaires	165
5 Time Management Strategies to get More Done in Less Time	169
CHAPTER FOUR: SHARPENING FOCUS	**173**
14 Exercises To Develop Razor-Sharp Focus	174
The Crucial Link Between your Brain and your Belly	181
5 Ways to Develop Unwavering Self-Discipline	183

CHAPTER FIVE: GOAL SETTING FOR SUCCESS............. 187
    Concepts Associated with Goal Setting 188

    Forms of Goals 189

    10 Goal-Setting Techniques to Achieve your Goals Faster 189

    7 Things you Need to Know About Setting the Right Goals ... 193

    The Best Ways to Reward Yourself for Completed Goals....... 196

CHAPTER SIX: NEW YOU, NEW ROUTINES...................... 199
    8 Ways to Create Great Habits that Lead to Success 200

    9 Morning Routine to Make Every Day a Good Day............... 206

    6 Evening Routines to Ensure Tomorrow is just as Good as Today. 210

CHAPTER SEVEN: NO MORE OBSTACLES 213
    7 Ways to Conquer Your Fear of Failure 213

    7 Strategies for Defeating the Monster of Perfectionism 216

    7 Ways in Which Positivity can Manifest Success 219

    5 Empowering Mantras to Destroy Self-Sabotage and Start Getting Stuff Done. 223

CONCLUSION 226

Introduction

It doesn't matter what phase of your life you are currently in, or what profession you may find yourself.

The truth is that all of us are all trying to overcome procrastination in one way or the other.

We yearn to not only get results, but to get them fast. Results are good, but the faster they arrive, the better for us. And this is where procrastination comes in.

Most of us already have everything planned out. Our heads a bubbling with a lot of ideas and visions, and we want to get started as soon as possible, but procrastination holds us back from achievement. It is so subtle that you never know that you are being held back.

Most people who procrastinate actually end up completing their tasks before the deadline, but they mostly face the pressure of completing a job under pressure. A procrastinator is never satisfied with the completed job even when it was completed before the deadline. There will always be this fear that something was not done right. Procrastination forces you to live in anxiety and perpetual fear.

There is hope. The first step is to understand that there is a problem. A procrastinator that doesn't know that he/she procrastinates is on the way to the largest pitfall in the world. Knowing you have a problem is the beginning of the solution. Procrastination is tricky, but it can be understood. You only have to make up your mind that you want to understand. And that is what I will be helping you do in this book: understand procrastination.

Beat Procrastination

You can only break its stronghold only after understanding what makes it strong. There are little bits that can help you overcome procrastination. Do you know that the content of your stomach at any given point can have an effect on your productivity at that time? Surprising, right? But that is the case.

As you follow my guides in this book, I want to assure you that you are in safe hands. I am Ethan Grant, and I love to think as myself as a productivity agent. I am a leading speaker on the topic of productivity. I understand both the concept of productivity and procrastination, and I know how to switch them in a person.

There is something I refer to as the procrastinator psychology. It is so strong in procrastinators that they hardly ever know it exists. I will be revealing that to you during our journey through the pages of this book. I only ask that you stay with me and be as attentive and proactive to change as ever. I have designed this book in the simplest form possible so that it can benefit anyone who reads it. The steps listed are all practical ones, so you will have problems following them.

Toni Morrison noted in one of her books, "If you surrender to the air, you can ride it." There are a lot of possibilities in your life. The quantities of things you can achieve are quite overwhelming, but procrastination will never let you.

If you have ever sat down to imagine all the great things you COULD have done but didn't do, even though you are 100% sure you have all it takes, then, you should know you have a procrastination problem. But once this problem is overcome, a lot of possibilities begin to open up to you, things you had never imagined you could ever do.

The benefits of conquering procrastination are numerous. Just sit and try to imagine all of the fulfillment and purpose that could come to your life if you decide to take a step today and become productive in whatever field you may find yourself.

My productivity tips have touched lives in various places. I have people call and tell me some of the ways in which my teachings have affected their lives very positively. Over the years, I have toiled endlessly to produce some of the nuggets I will be sharing with you in this book. You should count yourself lucky because you will be receiving most of my life's work in the following chapters. These are nuggets that have changed lives and created a fresh path for people who had once been frustrated in their frustration.

Productivity is a blissful thing, but it has to be understood and respected before it can be applied. Of course, nothing good comes easy, so you will have to give the procedures in this book some time before you begin to reap the benefits. But I can assure you that if these principles are applied, there is nothing that will be able to stop your light from shining.

You might be asking, 'Why this book, out of all the other books that deal with the topic of procrastination?' The major aim of writing this book is to pour all of myself into these pages. You won't just be reading a book; you will be picking my brain and going away with wonderful knowledge.

I am a seasoned teacher, and I try to be as technical as possible with any of my written works. This is to make sure that my reader easily understands the information I am trying to pass across. If the communication gap is faulty, then, the whole writing venture is utterly pointless. It is this communication gap that I have tried to bridge in the best way possible. The method listed here are procedures that a determined person can use successfully without any stress.

Remember, Heaven only helps those who help themselves. Sitting under an apple tree does not mean you will go home with a basket full. You need to take action and plug down some for your satisfaction. Success is right there at the corner, but she will never come into your house until you ask her in. And, dear, she can be very selective, only listening to those who understand her principles.

Finally, remember that our world only belongs to action-takers. No real change can happen except you decide to take action. Action is the key ingredient in every success story. You have to begin to beat procrastination now before it snatches away your glorious destiny.

A productive lifestyle should be your major aim as you strive to become a better version of yourself. Begin to practice all the tips and guidelines provided in this book and don't falter. Results take time to come back, and it is only the steady that stand to reap the benefits of their labor. I hope you soon have a positive story to tell. Good luck as we dive in.

Chapter One: Quit Bad Habits Now

The Biggest Misconceptions about Laziness

Let's start by noting that laziness is not a sickness or a personality disorder; it is mostly something you have accepted for yourself. Laziness is something that slowly creeps towards you, entangles you, and gradually takes over your personality. It is very stealthy, and it works hand-in-hand with procrastination.

Think of laziness as a desire of the layperson. It is something you want to do, something you are very comfortable with. Although a lot of people might argue and talk about how much they hate laziness, deep down inside of them, there is a part of them that is comfortable with just lying around and getting nothing done. It is almost like an inner conflict with yourself. One part of you is begging you just to achieve nothing, while the other part knows and understands the repercussions of those actions.

Take note that laziness and rest aren't the same. You rest after completing a huge project, but when this rest continues for an extended time, then you know that there is a problem. Laziness can so eat up into a personality that it becomes part of their personality, a habit that they can do nothing about. And this is where it gets weird and dangerous. At this point, the individual might begin to see laziness as a disorder or a sickness, which in most cases, is wrong.

The habit of laziness can form from a variety of circumstances. It is even more active in adults who have somehow lost motivation to be adventurous and seek out new things in the world. Study the children around you. You hardly see a lazy one. They are always up and doing, looking for the next big adventure and discovery. And that is why life stays bright and true to them because they understand the rudiments of new things.

On the contrary, laziness in an adult can result because the older person believes he has seen enough of life and is now particularly unmotivated. This is laziness of the mind. Here, the individual in question is endowed with enough strength and energy to carry out the task, but because there is no zeal, the task remains undone. And laziness is blamed.

From another perspective, laziness can be said to be a variety of states which can be emotional or physical that can affect a person's zeal to get things done. For different people, there are different reasons why they are lazy. Sometimes, laziness can spring up in a hardworking individual all because of lack of interest. Imagine an extreme introvert and extreme extrovert, both planning for parties. One will definitely put in more effort into the preparation more than the other. Now it is not that the introvert is lazy, but introverts are generally people who do not like to invest in social activities.

But this shouldn't be an excuse to accommodate laziness. A person is never born naturally lazy, except if there is a sickness that naturally weakens the individual. Apart from that, laziness is learned or walked into and becomes a habit. The funny thing about laziness as a habit is that it continues to grow on you until it completely destroys all of your plans. Laziness is one aspect of your life that can affect another part of your life and ruin it with laziness. If you get away with laziness today, your mind will try to trick you into believing you will get away with it again until the devastating finally happens.

5 Reasons Why You Are Lazy And How To Fix Them

Many times, people have a bleak sense of the fact that laziness has finally crept into their life. It is no longer a question of 'Am I lazy?', but now 'Why am I lazy?' While this is a very important question, the answer to that question is not readily available except through a deeper search. There are various reasons why people end up lazy, and these reasons vary from individual to individual. Laziness can be caused by a wide range of external factors, including psychological.

A lot of revelation has been given on how to overcome laziness. Like other traits, laziness can be pulled off one's skin and replaced. Although this method works, most times the candidates applying them may drop back into laziness. But there is something quite deeper to the situation. You have to sit and understand the true cause of your own brand of laziness before a solution can be prescribed.

There are some generally identifiable causes of laziness in different individuals, no matter their personality differences. Some of these include:

1. **Being overwhelmed by the task at hand**.

Some people get overwhelmed by the size of the work required to complete a project. One method to get rid of this is to break down major tasks into smaller tasks, but even this itself can cause a person to ignore the task. Most times, people lack the knowledge required to go about breaking down a task. So, they just forget the task and leave it hanging. This form of laziness mostly has to do with mental capability. It is laziness that is formed because an individual cannot do the mental exercise required to understand the task at hand.

This task will require an insane amount of research, materials collection, and all other requirements. But the solution here is to learn the skills involved in breaking down a task into smaller tasks. It is not a skill that one is born with. It is developed over time, with constant practice. If you have identified this kind of laziness in your life, it is time you put effort into learning how to deal with large projects and handle it in parts, one at a time.

2. Unidentified Purpose

Unless you have established the reason why the completion of a particular task will be important to you, your mind will never put the body to the task of completing the job. When there is no clear-cut purpose, there will hardly be any motivation to complete the task. Laziness easily seems to be a safe haven for people without a clear-cut purpose to pursue.

Once a person becomes plagued with such a form of laziness, there will be no zeal to act. All that they will be looking for is a form of escape, something that will relieve them of the thought of purposelessness. If you discover that you fall into this category of laziness, the solution will be to find something that motivates you. Find something that will make you want to act. Before you start any task, sit, and list out all of the benefits you can get when the task is finally complete. This will provide you with some motivation to get the job to the next level.

3. A need to produce a perfect job

Beat Procrastination

For a perfectionist, the rule is to get it done to 100% excellence or leave it undone. While this can sometimes be a very admirable trait necessary to produce the best results from a task, it can sometimes dampen a perfectionist's zeal to work. A perfectionist will spend hours and days gathering and perfecting the material requires to start up a task. The non-perfectionist, on the other hand, has already begun with what he has and has made progress. In time, he will be through with the job, putting the finishing touches to perfect the job as well as he could.

Perfectionists always get frustrated easier while working on a task because attaining perfection is never an easy task. There will always be factors on the ground that ensure that the work never attains perfection. The fear of making mistakes is another factor that holds perfectionists from starting up a task. This happens most especially when there is a portion of the job that they are not fully capable of carrying out. So, to prevent mistakes, they don't even start at all. While this might not outrightly translate into laziness, when it continues to build up, the person can begin to lose the zeal to work.

You can curb the effects of this perfectionist lifestyle by understanding that perfection is not attained in one go. It takes time to get something to be as good as you may want it to be. And that is the beauty of working on something, to put in more and more until you create something of quality. Quality takes time and effort. The joy is in the process of completing the job, and you will be fully rewarded when it is achieved. Understand that there is a time to set aside your perfectionist mindset and try to get things done, even if you are not too confident in your ability to complete the given task. Don't be scared that people will look at you differently when you fail. They, too, have failed before, so you shouldn't mind their glances. Just do what needs to be done.

4. Accepting laziness

There is a kind of laziness that is inhabited, laziness that you can speak yourself into. Some people have never put their minds into achieving something tangible, such that they don't even have an idea of what it is to be productive. It is more like a state of complacency and inactivity. These have a mentality that before a task can be carried out, it has to be fun and enjoyable, so whenever they are faced with a tedious task, they blank out and look for ways to escape. Things that do not fall into the enjoyable category are left for later, and then later, and finally later until they are never done.

Having these thoughts once in a while is completely normal. That is just the way your body works. But if it keeps on recurring over and over, then you know that they are a problem with your work ethic. Your body only wants to enjoy itself, which is wrong. There should be times when your body will be disciplined and made to get the job done. These thoughts can, in some ways, block your ability to produce something worthwhile, something that can be appreciated.

Strip your mind of these kinds of thoughts and get to work. See yourself as someone who has to achieve. Action taken now is always the best, and it will lead to the most satisfying rewards.

5. Health conditions

Like has been noted earlier, there is a kind of laziness that is caused by physical ailments or sickness. If you find out that you easily feel tired and there is never any motivation for you to work, then you should consider having yourself medically tested. These sicknesses hardly ever reveal themselves until it is quite late, but your body responds to them early enough, and it is left to you to detect these responses. One of such ways the body responds is to feel tired to help you conserve energy. Yet that shouldn't be the case. All of these could be as a result of a thyroid disorder. These thyroid problems could lead to diabetes, heart diseases, and other sicknesses that could weaken the body.

6 Ways to Overcome the Lazy Brain

When laziness becomes attached to a person, it can also affect their brain and make it lazy too. Your brain and your mind, most times, work hand-in-hand. And once one of them begins to accommodate the notions of laziness, the other is instantly affected. This is known as mental laziness.

Mental laziness can present itself in a variety of ways. For one thing, mental laziness can appear in the form of a disorganized and scattered mindset. Your mental faculty will always be in disarray, producing a lot of varying thoughts that mostly have no meaning. Most of these thoughts that occur as a result of the mental disarray are:

- Negative thinking.

The mind is mostly conditioned to think about the wrong things about life, always to ruminate and consider the things that have gone wrong. How do you expect to produce results when your mind is clogged with such thoughts? It will be very hard to achieve that. These negative thoughts can build up and affect you mentally, psychologically, and physically. Once your lazy brain tells your body that it is sick and it cannot perform, your body obeys and falls into laziness.

- Missing the most important things in the picture

A mind flooded with thoughts is a mind that will always be in a panic. Nothing ever stays stable. This can kind of thinking will always draw you into yourself, causing you to miss the things right in front of you.

Some of the ways in which you can control this lazy brain and bring it to book include:

1.   Guard your mind

Be a gatekeeper for all of the thoughts that pass through your mind. Observe the thoughts as they come and go and try to figure out the pattern in which they occur. You will be able to identify the negatives and positives. Probe yourself and find out why negative thoughts have become incessant. There may be small reasons lurking around, which you may need to fix. It could be anxiety, fear of failure, or mental stress.

2.   Pay attention to each thought.

As the thoughts come to your mind and try to produce laziness, pay attention to each and every one of them and find their root. If you are anxious about something, then find out why anxiety occurs in the first place. If you are stressed out and can't perform optimally, then try to find out how to combat this stress and restore your body to its normal functioning state. Eliminate these thoughts one by one and reduce the power of the lazy.

3.   Don't look for an escape.

Most people are always on the lookout for things that will help them escape the present and live in a parallel universe of entertainment. While it is OK to seek some form of escape from the hustle and bustle of life, it should be checked if it becomes too much. If you find out that you are that kind of individual that relies heavily on entertainment to escape and avoid the 'disturbances' in your life, you will notice that your mind will soon begin to experience deterioration.

There are other forms of escapism that people employ to release themselves from the grip of their lives. These recreational drugs only offer you short-term pleasure and heightened consciousness. Once it wears off, you are faced with the same issue that you had been trying to escape from. Your best option if to face whatever it is head-on and conquer it once and for all.

4.   Stay Mindful

Being mindful entails paying full attention to the things around you, both those that have to do with your mental state and those that have to do with the physical world around you. Don't let anything, no matter how small and infinitesimal it may be, pass you by. Enjoy life yet probe yourself and identify reasons why you enjoy certain things. While doing this, make sure to allow your mind some room for exploration. Allow your mind to wander a little, but don't allow it to travel too far lest you lose it.

5.   Get Organized

Disorganization easily results in clutter, and clutter in any form is not only a distraction but a huge wet blanket. Having your personal space clogged with clutter can result in loss of motivation. A clean space always invites you to work, to get something done. A disorganized space, on the other hand, pushes you away and tells you nothing can be done.

Try to observe it for yourself. How do you feel walking into the kitchen and meeting a pile of plates waiting for you in the sink? It is natural that you would want to attend to that before putting else on fire. The mind is always more comfortable and able to organize itself to produce whenever it is presented with a clean space.

6. **Seek help when necessary**

There is always help for you in trying to cure your mind of laziness. All you have to is to search for it. Sometimes you might not be able to get over a distraction or temptation to stay lazy single-handedly, but with the help of others, you will find it easy to do. There will naturally be this fear to meet people for help. This might be because of an unpleasant experience in your past, but it is a necessary skill to be learned, especially when struggling with something as addictive as laziness. A little practice may be needed to acclimatize you with the basics of finding help.

7 Terrible Habits that Keep you from Success

To live a life of productivity is to become successful in whatever you may find yourself doing. And habits themselves are some of the factors that build up to produce success. It is our habits that define us that make us who we are, either as success stories or as a failure. This is why it is necessary that one builds the perfect habits to enable success. Sadly, most people have spent their lifetime building habits that foster failure and push them further away from success. Here, I will be highlighting some of those habits that could hinder your success.

Beat Procrastination

1. **Inability to say 'no.'**

Sometimes you should be the bad guy and do some rejections. Not everything you are invited to participate in should be participated in. If you find it hard to say no and not feel guilty about it after, you will realize that you have stressed both your body and your soul. Also, if you keep on saying yes to everything, you will have an overwhelming schedule, which can turn out to be disastrous too.

Research has linked depression to an inability to say no because you will soon find out that you can no longer control yourself. Not saying no can derail you from your main goal and have you chasing something else simply because someone else had cajoled you into doing that.

2. **Fear of risks**

Play it smart, but don't play it safe. That is something I love to tell my students. It is natural to nurture some fear about your future, but you should never allow it to affect your work and the decisions you make. To fear risks is to ensure that you never get anything tangible. The best things will always elude you. And no matter how much you fear risks, that thing you fear will still befall you one day, so it is best to take the risk anyway. Take risks and fail and know that at least you learned something new. That is the beauty of life, to explore and discover new things.

3. **Held back by your past**

They say, "let bygones be bygones," and I couldn't agree more. Forget the thing in your past, the things of failure, and the things of success. Success, too, has a way of holding you back from achieving more. If you have achieved it before, then, you should forward and try to conquer more. Don't allow yesterday's success to prevent you from doubling your efforts and doing more. The same goes for failure too. The best thing you can do for yourself if to bury things of the past and look forward to the future.

4. **Building your life on mere talk**

This habit is deadly. It is for people who will spend most of their time talking about a vision instead of actually getting to work to make it happen. Talk is good, but the action is better. Do you know what is best? Getting to action immediately. Don't allow the sweet stories in your mouth clog up your mind until you begin to ignore the main work that has to be done. Talk is cheap, and action is expensive. Don't live a cheap life. It is dangerous.

5. **Playing blame games**

Blame is a heavy burden, and it is a beautiful thing to get it off your shoulders. You instantly experience freedom, and you can go back to relaxing. It stays sweet until it becomes too late when you finally discover what the damage of throwing blames has cost you. If you are to be blamed, there is no need to reject the blame for the sake of temporary freedom. Accept your blame and move forward with it. Instead of making excuses and trying to free yourself, try finding out why that venture failed in the first place. Throwing blame around is a recipe for more failure.

6. **Lack of self-discipline**

Self-discipline is simply obeying yourself as your own boss. Self-discipline is stooping low so that you are humble enough to listen to your own self. You should be able to talk yourself towards success and out of failure. In fact, you can never succeed if you have not learned how to scold yourself when necessary. Apart from that, you should fear the deadlines you place. There should be punishments for not completing a task at the right time. These are some of the things that self-discipline entails. In the end, it is all about being your own toughest master and teacher.

7. **A competitive mindset**

Subscribing to healthy competition is suitable for your development, but when competition begins to lead to envy and low self-esteem, it becomes dangerous. Your major completion should be yourself. Improve yourself irrespective of the success of others or what they are embarking on at the moment. Allow other people's success to become a motivation to drive to work, not to drive you insane. Stay in your lane, but ensure that you make that lane the best it can be.

Chapter Two: Firing Up A Motivated Mind

You might be surprised that, while things might get tough, only now, you lose the drive to continue because it is just about you. Of course, the only "being" you see around is your inner self. And even your inner will to push forward has been stricken with a deadly disease I call frustration.

Do not fret! You eventually get to that stage. In fact, it is a big sign that you are progressing. It shows that you have scaled through the starter's level. Although the progress might appear slow and it might not mean much compared to the goal you have set to achieve, you are now in a position where you need to get motivated.

Be careful not to express this feeling of frustration into your daily life. The consequential effect is that nothing will seem to work for you. Why? Because you have preconditioned it as a reality to live with.

Two things might set in, discouragement and procrastination. Discouragement because you are not sure if it's going to work. And procrastination because your progress is slow. Neither of these is a deal to settle for, and other harmful things might follow.

This chapter will explore all you need to know on how to keep going.

Which Type of Procrastinator are you?

It will be interesting to note the importance of productivity at our workplace and in our daily lives. But one thing that destroys our creative ability to do more is procrastination. Procrastination is simply the act of pushing the accomplishment of things to the future; things you consider of less value in your present moment.

Beat Procrastination

We all have been in this pool before. Admitting this fact doesn't present it as a good habit to do. Although prioritizing might redefine the content of the tasks pushed to the future, it only shows that we have been able to identify the root of age-old difficulties. Some might tend to shift responsibility to another time because they feel that they are incapable of doing such a task. Others might just be to fulfill another act of laziness.

1. The Evader

There are times when we are at our best to accomplish a task. But sometimes, we just decide not to continue because we worry that we can't do it. Self-doubt then kills creativity in us. You are scared that you might flop, and the only thing that comes to your mind is to push it forward. No one will argue the fact that it is good to recognize our limitations and weakness. It is also necessary that you don't allow it to hold you back.

Build a sense of importance

Understand the value attached to the task you avoid. See those values as commitments that need life support. Of course, you are the one who secures its existence by accomplishing it. And since life support is not a decision to avoid, your tasks shouldn't also. You may tend to compare each of those jobs you push further as your heartbeat. As much as our heartbeat is essential in the future, it is considered as of greater importance for the present also.

Breaking out of the evader

- Outline a positive outcome

Create enough reasons not to avoid the task. The joy of achievement alone should be a constant motivation to spark you up. While you have been a continuous benefactor of the satisfaction and pleasure derived from not doing it immediately, you can also get that fulfillment when you think of it positively.

- Gear up your will

Everything inside you must receive the right knowledge to do things quickly. And the good thing about willpower is that you are the best influencer.

- Start in pieces

Work can be overwhelming sometimes; but with strategy, it will become interesting. Break down the process of completing the task into parts. Don't think of achieving it in a stretch. Allot each piece with a time limit, say for 5 minutes (you are in control here). You might need to declutter your bedroom. Give three minutes to arrange your sneakers and two minutes to sort out a tie. Going with this flow makes the job quite more manageable and exciting.

2. The Stickler

Excellence is a virtue that should be seen in everyone; but it shouldn't affect the completeness of a job. Some people are stuck in the circle of bringing out the best in everything they do. They can't do less until they are satisfied that the work is world-class.

No one is negating the just essentials of doing things in the best way; it proves the importance of productivity. But understand that in many cases, the attention required for such tasks needs to be well monitored; and so, we tend to push it forward because we are overwhelmed. There is this fear of low standard that denies them to start off immediately.

Breaking out of the stickler
- Do the analysis

Mathematics wouldn't be necessary here, but you can think of doing the arithmetic of the last job you did. Ask yourself different questions ranging from when you started to how did you complete it. Was there any consequential effect attached to it? Were you able to attain a 100% success rate? Was there any reward of internal satisfaction to this? What outlook did it give your job? It is more likely that you have been too hard on yourself to perfect your next task, and that's why you want to fix the slightest details.

- Have a clear intent

Understand the nature of the work to be done. The technicalities, modules of operation, design outlay, and presentation. Be sure to have a clear definition of what you need to achieve. When your purpose is clear, you will not be distracted.

- Define your satisfaction

A functional analysis would make this step easier for you. Once you have been able to itemize what your happiness is, looking for it in every job you do would not be a problem again. Your satisfaction might come when you achieve, say, the right mix of color in your interior designs.

3. **The Cluttered Brain**

Yes, clutter! It might be true that we are really busy with many things to do. Ranging from work to social group activities, religious commitment, health and safety checks, family upkeep, and so many more engaging routines. Multiple office tasks alone at your workplace might be a threat to prioritize your daily job. It then becomes a problem to choose the right task to do at the moment. And when this gets too much for us, we tend to do some tasks and push others to the future. Sometimes, our mental state is as busy as our workload that we get confused from within first, then the reality of the physical adds insult to injury. It is apparent that you are occupied with many things to do, and the slightest time to rest is also used to think. You would agree with me that those thoughts aren't as productive as they should.

Breaking out of the cluttered brain
- Set priorities

Identify the most relevant job at hand and do them immediately. Don't ever get overwhelmed when minor tasks seem to be the large chunk of the situation. Create an express list of your routine tasks. Do the ones you feel is both necessary and urgent right away, and steadily complete others.

- Determine a deadline

As much as the job is essential, it is vital to set a time limit for each of your task. Taking too much time on a particular problem leaves others piling. Note that your time limit must be achievable. Since most of your works are routinely done, devise a strategy to simplify the process.

- Work with facts

Seek the counsel of the experts on specific tasks. Taking a step like this gives you an edge to succeed at a faster rate. Work with proven facts and figures from professionals and ease your workload burden.

- Delegate responsibilities

You don't have to necessarily do all the work. Seek the help of a colleague or, better still, allow your office assistant to do a part of the job. Be careful, though, in delegating power. Ensure that you take the critical decisions and monitor the progress of any delegated duties.

4. Carefree

These people do not see any reason to do a particular task at its proposed time. They feel that there is enough time to do the job. Fun is being derived from this act, and nothing seems to make more sense than taking hands-off work.

Remember when you needed to write a college report for a field trip, and the experience from this exercise encouraged you to plan for the next one? What happened is that you spent a lot of time fantasizing about the next trip but not into writing the report. So, the time meant for the critical task of getting the description ready was used for something else which might not be as important presently.

A fraction of this group believes that they are most effective when the deadline is close. So, they feel pressured to put in their best at the very last hour.

Breaking out of the carefree
- Do statistics for arithmetic

You might not be familiar with this principle. It's simple. Since you really don't see a reason to do the most crucial task at the moment, try applying the same principle to what you would have done at that moment. Try procrastinating your fun-filled activities. Experimenting on this will give you another sense of urgency to undertake tasks.

- Count the effects

You might need to be truthful to yourself here: What you really want is fun. But how much has this fun cost you? Think of a greater sense of accomplishment you would have had if you don't push the task to the future. There is no harm in attempting something good, so give it a try.

- Examine your triggers

You might not be aware that the source of your procrastination is not really you, but what you do at some point. Your environment might be a trigger. Do a brief examination of the things you do and see if you can do them in another way. Apply the same principle for your tasks too. It might interest you to discover what pushes you to procrastinate.

5. The fantasizer

If you belong to this group, it means you have spent a lot of time having plans but didn't take any constructive step to accomplish it. It looks quite easy to talk about reading five chapters of a book per day. In fact, you might have initiated this whole idea to your colleagues, but the stage of presenting it was the last effort made to achieve it. Understand that a proposed action without a constructive strategy remains a fantasy.

Breaking out of the fantasizer

- Understand goal setting

Starting with a plan is not a wrong move, just that the approach to achieve it must be accurately spelled out. Goal setting takes a commitment of not giving up even in the face of distractions. You will need to take every suggestion given in Chapter Five of this book seriously.

- Start small

There is no need to rush to get to the height you have always imagined. Take your time to do your task. Remember what you want to achieve will not come automatically.

- Get real

Stop wasting time on what is not achievable. If what you have always planned to do is unrealistic, its time to cut them short and get real.

10 Must-Know Hacks for Mind-Blowing Motivation

Excellence is a thing to think of when aiming at achieving goals. Lots of factors would need attention to actualize this, and one of them is motivation. Motivation is that force that keeps you going in the face of challenges and distractions. To meet your targets, you would need to keep moving to enhance your productivity level and boost your performance.

1. Begin Little

One big killer of achievement is when you don't see yourself doing more, especially the way you have fantasized it. It wouldn't come as you thought. Understand that what should matter most to you whenever you are starting something new is progress.

It might look tiresome because you feel you are not moving at the same pace as others'. That might be another mistake also. This is you doing your own thing, so you don't have any obligation to work at anyone's speed. Checking other people's progress should inspire you to do more, not to enslave you into regret.

The reality of a long-term goal is that it requires a long period to be achieved. So take it slow and steady until you finally meet your targets. You don't need to fret.

2. Identify a Strong Purpose

You shouldn't undertake anything when you have not outlined the intent. It is necessary because this will serve as a reminder any time you want to give up. Your purpose should be firm and essential to you. This assurance is what upholds your willpower.

Your intent might stem from your childhood experience, goal setting, career choice, family background, and so on. Whatever it is, it must be convincing to you. Be careful not to be enticed by the environmental factors. Don't take a course of action because that is the trend in your immediate environment. Be sure that you have thought about it very well and you are ready to go through it.

3. Design a Structure for your Goals

You need to differentiate yourself from everyone else. Remember that your intentions have a deadline, so nothing should distract you from fulfilling it. Create a guide that will help you focus. It can be an express outline of your targets or a picture containing what you want to achieve. Doing this brings clarity of purpose. You then know every input/resource needed to achieve success.

With a structure, you will be able to track your progress at every point in time. If it is necessary to report to anyone, your composition would have mapped it out. You wouldn't get tired of achieving an outstanding result because your progress is evident. Having a well-defined structure makes you advance in the essential details. It is a sure model for motivation.

4. Add Fun to your Task

Beat Procrastination

No one is encouraged to do more when everything seems tedious, especially when it is a routine task. Position your job as part of your life that deserves happiness. And an excellent way to stay happy while doing your work is when you add fun to it. You don't have to be rigid here, and your job might not necessarily be a treat.

Also, don't forget that discipline should not be a lamb to sacrifice for pleasure. Play your favorite playlist while you type and enjoy the rhythm. You may also decide to chat with your colleague during your break. Speak lavishly about what makes the job interesting.

5. Look Out for your Tribe

Tribe here means people of the same kind. It might be a colleague that has decided to be on the same course of action with you. You might have decided to write a review for five international magazines on a particular theme. Check someone around you who have made the same decision too.

You will get more inspired because you are sure that you are not alone on this journey of success. Seeing the other person(s) creates a mindset of competition. Make it more fun when you meet with them by challenging your abilities. Your aim here is not to feel awkward even if you don't meet the target given to you. The teamwork spirit should get you going.

6. Avoid Negative Thoughts

Naturally, diverse ideas will flow through your mind, whether you are doing well or not. But you can sieve whatever comes to your mind. Be in control of what dominates your thoughts, especially negative ones. A better way to maintain good ideas is to have positive affirmations whenever a bad one flashes in your mind. You might be thinking of not achieving the task because you feel you are incapable. Tell yourself that "I am not deficient of abilities, and I will have productive and outstanding results."

7.   Learn more

Task yourself to learn about a particular task. The good thing about knowledge is that it set you further beyond expectation. Many people have actually gone through what you are thinking of doing. Read about them. Learn the different challenges they faced and how they overcome them. Reading their stories will position you to have extensive experience as you won't need to fall victim to the circumstances. Read newspapers, magazines, and blogs; watch videos, and get yourself inspired by your discoveries.

8.   See a Professional

Their job is to guide you through extraordinary sessions. Your aim here is not to limit yourself to what you hear. An encounter with the experts makes the job more personal. You will be able to relate your fears, frustrations, and challenges with an open mind. At the end of the day, you must have been held accountable for the procedural counsel. You could also sharpen your leadership skills with a professional. And if the success of what you want is a priority, don't think about the cost attached to seeking the help of a professional.

9.   Step Back Frequently

Working smart is the key to a successful work outcome. You don't have to get stuck over a task for too long just because you want to find a solution. Restore your mental capabilities by taking breaks. Your health is most valuable when you need to get going. You would agree that you are less productive whenever you spend more time than necessary. You might be trying to design a book cover, but it seems the dots are not connecting. Leave the job for a while. Take a walk down the street or probably surf the internet. During that break period, your brain and other parts of your body would have been refreshed, leaving you better than before.

10. Live Healthily

No one can take care of you better than you. Look out for nutrient-giving foods. You might consider eating vegetables and fruits, depending on your diet. Taking water frequently is quite healthy. The focus here is that your physical body must be able to sustain every activity you intend to do. Living in sickness is enough discouragement to perform any task.

The Fixed Mindset vs the Growth Mindset

The subject of mindset is important because what we make of it determines our productivity level and success rate. Mindset is the collection of ideas (stemming from personal to environmental, cultural, and spiritual experience), assumptions, beliefs, and thoughts held up to become a constituent part of inclination, interpretations, disposition, and mental habit. It is then crucial to master the art of mindset both for personal or professional use. The effect of mindset is shown at the behavioral level and creates a rigid perspective about life in general.

The Fixed Mindset

As the name implies, a fixed mindset holds that their daily-life attributes are static traits, and therefore cannot be modified. People with this mindset focus more on what they can do as fuelled by their intelligence, ability, and talents. Any effort that leads to success is not an option to them. They somewhat vouch on their talent alone instead of adopting strategies to improve and build it. You might have seen people who have limited themselves on the extent of performance; those already have a perspective of "I can't change."

An example of someone with a fixed mindset is one who believes that he is an athlete because he can sprint to some extent. The mindset would be known during training sessions. If he insists that he can't break the track record but can only maintain his current streak of performance, then he is susceptible to be one.

The fixed mindset does not see opportunities to get better at what they do, and they put no effort to improve. You may have come across people who are dogmatic about using some modern facilities just because they were raised by their grandparents, and must have been misinformed. Whenever there is any change, then it is not for them.

Also, consider when a student is taught how to solve a particular problem in Mathematics. If the facilitator adds variables to the question, then explaining it conventionally becomes a problem (something a fixed mindset will give up on because he felt the other way around is the best way to solve it), so, he gives up.

He could have accepted his weakness in not knowing the problem and then looked for a way around it. The change in the question posed a threat to him already, and he felt helpless, and that was enough reason to give up. If he were asked why he gave up, it would be easy to point fingers, go defensive, and retaliate.

The Growth Mindset

A growth mindset accommodates changes to improve skills and qualities through perseverance, dedication, and effort. People with this mindset believe in all-around development by building strengths and abilities, not just where they feel they have the ability.

These people have an understanding that learning can be developed with persistence. Although when failure comes, it is with an understanding that it can get better, and not an avenue to shy away. They have an insight into the realities of possibilities.

People with a growth mindset are most likely to work at their full potential because challenges do not make them stop, but instead put in more effort. For example, one out of five foreign students in a German class has difficulties in the language. A growth mindset will not get discouraged because he didn't meet the standard of others, but will understand that he just needs to give more effort. Patience will be another thing to take note of here.

5 Tips for Developing a Mindset That Brings You Success

1. Create a Platform to Learn Something Different Every Day

The dependency of fixed traits will not breed a world-class result. Take time to speak with a professional in the line of your strength and ability. There is always a better version of your power. The expert should be able to guide you effectively and push you to do the right thing at every needed moment. Take the pain of learning and doing something different from your immediate talent every day. You may also consider reading about what you learn online or join a friend who wants to learn the same with you

2. Expand your Learning Experience

It is super cool to hear of one's assessment from people. But when it becomes a habit, then you need to be wary. You don't have to focus on getting approval from people around you. It does not matter what they think or say about what you do. Channel that energy into learning. Learning should be your priority and follow the procedures patiently. Bear in mind also that education is a process, and it may not come easy as you would expect. The learning experience will keep you going to achieve great results.

3. Reference Weakness

You must know where the problem is coming from. It might be triggers or just your community of friends. Enough of the excuses for failure and dejection! Embrace your weakness by acknowledging it. This will be the first step in liberating yourself to the world of growth.

4. Be Open to Different Eventualities

Challenges would definitely come, but you have to be prepared for it. Prepare your mind to see the goodness in every difficulty. Learn to weigh your options. Always consider using "what if." You might have decided to read for three hours a day, and it seems unachievable. Ask questions and challenge your routine. What if I have not been following my guide? What if I need to be more specific? What if I need to take breaks? What if I check my diet? What if I read about people who have done the same thing?

5. Reflect Daily

You should be in charge of disbursing the truth to yourself. Have time to meditate on your course of action. You might find it interesting to do this at night when you are done with the work for the day. Analyze those thoughts that have limited you to underperform and how you can overcome them.

Chapter Three: Getting The Job Done

Productivity entails a lot of things, and one of the most important of them is about getting things done. As easy as it may look, a lot of people still have problems getting things done at the right time and in a complete manner.

This is where the understanding of productivity comes into play. To be productive is to understand tips and techniques and know-how to apply them accordingly. Productivity works like a system, but it doesn't just go into action.

In this chapter, I will be guiding you through some of these factors that can help you become more productive. The techniques and tips I will be revealing to you will yield viable results for you if only you decide to use them unflinchingly.

11 Essential Techniques to Power Up Your Productivity

To understand ways to build productivity, it is necessary that one understands the meaning of productivity. They are many misconceptions about the term, and if they are not handled, the whole essence of this chapter will never be accomplished.

First of all, bear it in mind that productivity isn't only about ticking boxes off your to-do list. It is more than that. Productivity, in this sense, basically entails getting the right things done in the right time frame in the most effective way possible. Having the perfect system to help you boost productivity is very necessary for both your work life and your family life. You definitely stay ahead of things when you understand the mechanisms that fuel productivity.

Beat Procrastination

The building blocks of productivity is in setting up realistic goals and achieving them one step at a time. At the end of the task, you should be able to ask yourself, "Did I do something meaningful with the space of time allocated to me?" If the answer is yes, then congratulations are in order. You have been productive.

One major reason why people fail at being productive is that they have too much going on for them. Being able to select the right task for you and going after them headlong is a very special and important skill that you should learn. There a whole lot more techniques that are quite important when trying to become more productive, and I am going to walk you through some of them. Follow these techniques closely, and watch productivity take a great leap in your life.

1.   The Eisenhower Matrix

You will most definitely need a pen and paper for these techniques because you will have to draw out a quadrant. The first two quadrants at the top of the four squares will be tagged "very important." The next two underneath will be tagged "less important." But the first two quadrants from the left side will be tagged "urgent" while the next two quadrants at the right will be tagged "less urgent."

After that is complete, you can now begin to sort all your tasks into the boxes. There are those that will fall under "very important" but "less urgent." Others will be "very urgent" but "less important." It is all about understanding how to place each task. Every task that falls into "very important" and "very urgent" should be the ones that you will face quickly. Those definitely carry a lot of weight. On the other hand, those that fall into "less urgent" and "less important" are the ones that can be left for later. Assigning your tasks in all of these boxes will help you with your decision making.

2. The 80/20 rule

The idea of the 80/20 rule comes from a business model. What it means is that 80% of all your profits come from lesser than 20% of your customers and business partners. With that, it is necessary that you know how to treat this 20 % so that they stay and keep providing you with 80% of your profit.

Bring that into your daily life and see how it translates. Notice how just a few things you do actually have a lot of impact on your life. Less than 20% of your everyday activities are enough to have a real influence on your life over a long period of time. It would make sense to place a strong focus on that 20 % so that more meaningful impact can be generated.

3. The Five Majors

This concept was developed by the CEO of Stack Overflow, and its concepts encourage that one person should never have more than five activities on their to-do list at any point in time. Keep your lists short and try to achieve everything on the list with a short period so that you can add more activities to the list and go ahead. You should be working on at least two activities on your list, the next two should be in a queue, and the last one should be a secret task that only you know about, something you must have challenged yourself to do.

4. Exercise your Body and Mind

Exercise frees your body and gets it ready to perform. Exercise in this form does not only have to do with the body alone but also the mind. While the body profits from your physical exercise, the mind profits from mental exercise. Mental exercise helps you to open up your mind and allow your imaginations to run wild, which is quite beneficial to your productivity.

5. A Break will Help you

Some of the most productive people understand the power of breaks. Not only will they help your body relax and feel out new ways to relax and get things done, but they will also allow your mind to re-strategize plans. Have you noticed how the best ideas come to you when you have totally forgotten about the job? Yes, that is your brain working on its own, undisturbed by the stress of your coaxing and anxious mind. Instead of working for long stretches, set a timer and get things done in little bits. They will cumulate into one big success story.

6. Shun Multitasking

There are people who have optimized their bodies and minds for multitasking. It is quite easy for them. That is rarely ability, too. No one is saying you can learn it now, but don't gamble with it just yet. Take time to study yourself and find out how good you are with multitasking. Chances are, you are not very good; so it will be best for you not to venture there. Nothing kills productivity faster than a person trying to multitask. And in the real sense of things, multitasking is a form of distraction in itself. Your mind remains divided throughout the process. Just focus on one job at a time and see how far you can go with that.

7. Love the Things you Do

This is not easy to do, especially for people who have found themselves in jobs that they are not happy with. If you are not happy, then it means you do not love what you do, which leads to frustration. If you are not happy, it is better you leave and find something that gives you fulfillment. The truth is that you can hardly be productive doing something you do not love. If you love it, your mind will no longer view it as work, and it will be easier for you to perform the said tasks.

8. Strangle your Distractions

Getting rid of glaring distractions is key to increasing productivity. Every entertainment in your life is there to reduce your productivity level. Once you understand that and deal with them squarely, it will be easier to overcome them as they arrive. Tell your mind to focus on the essentials and not look sideways to the non-essentials. The funny thing is that your mind obeys you, and it, too, would like to see a specific task completed.

Find a quiet place where you can work, a place where you are sure you will not be distracted. This is the first step in dealing with distractions. If you have created a list, then tell yourself that there will be no fun for you until you have accomplished about three things on that list. Breaking our tasks into smaller bits always helps.

9. Complete the Most Important Tasks First Thing in the Morning

The best time to complete your most intimidating tasks is early in the morning when your mind is most vibrant and ready to perform. Don't put off your task until it becomes late, and then you find yourself rushing the task to complete the task. Begin before your mind starts to slack and watch yourself progress even before the day goes halfway. Completing the most taxing activities early in the morning will give your mind and body a kind of positive push to keep trying harder.

10. Create a Schedule

Don't just rush into things without a plan. A schedule will help you to streamline your activities and keep you more focused while helping to eliminate distractions. But don't forget to create time for rest and pleasure in your schedule. If not, it will never be a workable one. Take off whole hours to get yourself together and replenish your mind.

11. Reward yourself

If you have achieved anything that marks you off as productive, then you should reward yourself. Your reward can come in any form, but make sure it is something you will enjoy, something you will thank yourself for. Having rewards set in place will give you something to look forward to asking you try to complete the task as fast as possible.

10 Secrets Behind Productivity According to the World's Billionaires

There is no better place to get advice than from the best of the best, some of the most productive people in the world who are billionaires. It is not easy to control your environment, but you can learn how to do so, and this is something that billionaires are quite good at. You should sit down and try to learn from them.

The world has more than 1500 billionaires, and most of them are quite effective at time management and productivity. Don't get it twisted. These people live the same kind of lives as you. They receive thousands of emails every day that require sorting. They have thousands of employees in their payrolls, and they also have a lot of decisions to make every day. Have you ever wondered how they manage to stay on top and achieve so much in such little time? How they choose the things that are important and those that can be left for a later time? These are men and women who have built their wealth systems in such a way that they receive in excess of $5000 every day. And productivity is something they don't joke with.

Here are some of the most outlined points that they listed as some of their most important:

1. You Don't Have to be Everywhere

The late Steve Jobs stated that to increase his productivity; he spent a lot of time streamlining the number of meetings and places he had to be per day. Some other billionaires stated that there is no need to attend a meeting or being in a place if you are sure that you won't make a lot of money from it, or talk about something really important. It is more important that you delegate someone to go on your behalf instead of presenting yourself at the venue. Most high-profile billionaires have described most meetings as a waste of time with people talking about irrelevant things.

2. Simplify your Calendar

Your calendar here refers to your schedule. Most billionaires advise that people learn to keep their calendar simple and decongested. Instead of having hundreds of things to be done in one week, try picking out a select few to be accomplished within that week and leave the rest for the next week. It is no good trying to stuff your schedule with lots of things and not achieving any of them in the long run.

3. Identify the Place Where you Perform Best

We are all different, and we all have different psychologies. Because of this, the areas where we most liable to perform best differ from person to person. Find your place and stick to it. What time of the day do you perform best? How should a surrounding be before you can get in the zone to work? For some people, a loud and noisy environment is the ideal place to work. For others, it will be a silent and very secluded environment where they will come in contact with very few people.

Once you find out what works best for you, build on it and enhance that environment. Some billionaires have thinking rooms built into their homes where they sit and think for hours on end; others travel to very secluded places where they can commune better with themselves. And all of these produce very wonderful results for different individuals, especially when they are practiced in the right way.

4. Keep your Focus on the Most Important Goals

There are goals, and there are GOALS. The key here is not allowing other less important goals to hold you back from achieving the main important goals. People who achieve a lot know how to set the most important goals and face them like their lives depend on it. This is not to say that you ignore your other dreams. Instead, keep your eyes on the big ones, those ones that will have the most positive impact in your life within the shortest time.

5. How Well are you Doing?

Billionaires are people that love to track their process on any project. Nothing is ever done just because it is done. They live their life intentionally and love to follow all of those intentions and see success. It is advised that you create metrics with which you can use to determine how good you are performing. Your metrics can be using a small book to write down everything you achieve or making use of software or apps that help to track process. With a fully tracked process, you will be able to look and improve your performances.

6. Take Advantage of all the People Around you

The people around you are some of your most important resources. It is quite neglected, but billionaires have always advised people to be more conscious of the people around them. If you are the kind of person who loves to work on your own and shut out other people, then you should learn to make some adjustments in your life. People are always around that can make your life more successful, and you should maximize them. Billionaires basically report that they recruit people to help them achieve their dreams and ideas. Getting to use people is to create more time for yourself. The job gets faster in a shorter time. The major problem is in finding competent people; but once you are able to scale that, you will have the most productive time of your life.

7. Technology is There for you

Renowned billionaires around the world are known for their love of technology. Look what Facebook did for Zuckerberg. Look at Steve Jobs, Bill Gates, and other selected ones. Sometimes technology is your best option. Technology gets it done easier and quicker.

Automation can work in any business as long as you are able to discover a way to introduce it into your business to help you work better. All you have to do is make sure you already have an efficiently working system before you incorporate technology into your work. If not, you might end up confusing yourself and achieving nothing.

8. Create habits that help your Productivity

Billionaires are people of practice; they know how to build positive habits that help them to become more productive. Some of them are known to be early morning people; others are known to be nocturnal animals. Billionaires know how to develop the perfect habits to help them out to become more productive.

9. Set Time for the Most Important Work

Remember that activity is not equal to productivity. Don't allow yourself to get drowned in the hustle and bustle of life. There should be a set time for you to carry out the most tasking of your activities.

Productive billionaires know that special time needs to be set aside to get the most important jobs done. During this time, there will be no calls, no emails, and no internet. It will be only you and the job right there in front of you.

10.   Recognize your Opportunities

Productive billionaires unsurprisingly have the best eyes suited for figuring the best opportunities that should be maximized. You will be tempted to take on every viable opportunity in front of you, but not all opportunities are for you. Take time to review all the opportunities in front of you and find the ones that best suit your skills and personality.

5 Time Management Strategies to get More Done in Less Time

There is something about time management you need to know: Time cannot be managed. Instead, you can only manage the events that occur within a period of time, giving the illusion that time has been managed. Every one of us has been provided with the same quantity of time, which is 24 hours per day and 7 days per week and so on. So, the question now is, how can you fit all of your activities into this period of time so that you come out with the utmost satisfaction and remain productive?

With this understanding, it is also necessary that you note that time is also a commodity. It can be sold and it can be bought. It can also be budgeted, and it can be used with wisdom and common sense. Another thing is that time management is an art that can be mastered.

Time management strategies are affected by different factors when they are applied by different individuals. Personality, will to achieve, and the level of discipline are some of the factors that can affect a person's ability to manage time. These strategies have been proven over time to help people with managing their time. Practice them and watch your life change.

1.   **Be Organized**

Disorganization and poor time management go hand-in-hand. Where one is present, the other manifests itself. Get rid of any form of clutter that may have besieged your life so that time will be spent more wisely.

There are simple ways in which you can achieve organization and a decluttered life. There are thousands of resources on the internet that can help you out, but the simple way out is to learn when to let go of things. Know what to put away and what to leave. Note that the clutter that is being referred to does not only have to do with the physical everyday clutter. There is also the mental clutter and digital clutter. All of these have a way of slowing you down and reduce your ability to manage time.

To get rid of mental clutter, make sure that your mind stays clear both emotionally and psychologically. An unstable mind is a distraction, which in turn deprives you of focus. Digital clutter, on the other hand, will mix up your files that will make you spend hours looking for a document. Deal with all of these individually and return your life to stability.

2.   **Identify and Deal with Time Wasters**

Your productivity and time management is affected by a lot of external factors controlled by the people and circumstances in your life at any given moment. These factors are some of the major causes of time wastage, as they have a way of affecting you without your knowledge. All that happens is that with time, you discover that you missed something somewhere. But you have the power to either increase or decrease their effect such that they are no longer capable of wasting your precious time. Some of these factors you should look out for include:

- Uninvited visitors or guests
- Unimportant emails and letters to be replied
- The internet (social media)
- Relationships
- Little pleasures

3. Is your Time Worth Anything?

Take a few minutes and try to take stock of your time. How much is it worth to you? If it is worth something, then how can it translate into productivity? Once you do this, you will find for yourself a sense of understanding that your time should be spent wisely because of its worth. When the value of a thing is unidentified, it is easy for it to be abused and misused. Create value for your time and don't allow that value to ever be reduced. If you are going to get distracted for 15 minutes, you should be able to determine how much you must have lost during those gone 15 minutes. With that in place, you will easily be able to organize your mind and get yourself to act.

4. Care for Yourself

Taking care of yourself is one major way in which you can avoid time wastage. Take time to relax your body, your mind, and your soul. Keeping your body and mind at its best helps you accomplish tasks even faster than usual. Find out what time of your day your body performs best and maximize those periods to the best of your ability.

Mismanagement of time can manifest as a result of bodily fatigue and sickness. Depression can also cause you to put off important activities, and this is why your mental health should also be checked from time to time. As I have noted before, take time to rejuvenate your mind and reward yourself whenever you are sure you have accomplished something noteworthy.

There should be a healthy balance in your life between your work and family. There can never be any form of real productivity without this balance in place. Instead, you will spend a lot of time thinking you are productive at work while your personal life experiences failure.

5.   **A Necessary Sense of Urgency**

To have a sense of urgency is to understand that there is no room for time wastage. It is to understand that speed is necessary when an opportunity presents itself. Develop the ability to take action and to take them very quickly. It is one thing to take the corresponding action, and it is another to take that action before it becomes too late. One thing that differentiates achievers from their opposites is their ability to take appropriate action sat the right time.

Chapter Four: Sharpening Focus

Awareness is a thing to remember when learning to get focused, whether on personal targets or on assigned duties. It is one of the tools leaders consider in achieving a massive turnout of success. The beginning of this consciousness positions leaders to direct the attention of people following them. To sustain this growth, the leader must focus on their care.

We must first know that getting focused is beyond filtering alternatives while paying attention to one. One could concentrate in diverse ways and for different purposes to pursue an available course. Being a leader here does not necessarily mean you lead in a position of authority, and you are not pushed to the thought of being one. Our priority is to ensure that you lead a proper life for yourself.

Remember that there is a larger world to give attention to; those things that connect you to the world. People following you (comprising of people you work with or for, the ones you mentor, and the ones you are accountable for) deserves attention too, and lastly, yourself.

Problems you complain of often might come from distraction, or maybe multitasking. With things ranging from meetings to work schedule, back-to-back reviews and presentations, and finally again to supervision, note how each day has become a mountain of workload. And you could barely have time to sort out your thoughts. This schedule would be reasonable if you are 100% sure of your success rate and might not need a rethink. But in the long run, you might break down both mentally and physically.

14 Exercises To Develop Razor-Sharp Focus

We would begin with those little daily tasks you often consider as of little importance. Expect to see a change as you hold the exercises with the utmost value. This mind will be the breakthrough to sustain the success of the activities.

1. **Learn your Work Structure**

Increase your focus rate by understanding the details of the job. Ask questions on what is unclear. Meet your supervisor or your direct superior and make clarifications. You might want to ask for a record of such a task that has been done before. Your inquisitiveness would clear the doubt that would have misled you. And will only make you look out for the excellent completion of the job. Your focus would now be sharpened as you can now comprehend every fragment of your work schedules.

2. **Arrange your Desk**

This exercise will deal with every distraction that might spring from clutter. Imagine your table is full of unfinished reports, seminar papers, minutes, and other relevant official documents. What happens is any time you see them gives you anxiety and worry. Fear tends to creep in.

Instead of allowing such unnecessary pressure from your mind, arrange or rearrange your desk as the case may be. Keep documents in their order of priority and gain some peace for your mind, if for nothing else. This action will allow you to be conscious of what is most significant at the moment, and you will be mindful of it.

3. **Stretch your Body**

Mental capability is not isolated from our physical components. Your hands, leg, even neck plays a lot of role in improving your productivity level. Note that I am not negating other parts of your body; neither do I underestimate their functions. Our attention here is the role each of your locomotive parts plays in revitalizing your body.

Practice twisting your fingers one after the other in a clockwise rotation. You need to be careful and gentle with this exercise so as not to injure yourself. Continue the rotation for five minutes and pay attention to the steady movement you are making. Fix your mind on all you notice, starting from the sound of the first two rotations to the unequal flow of the tip bone. You might see your veins and how your wrist tends to move with the spinning finger. Take time to do this with all your fingers with your mind focusing on the movement.

You might extend this practice to your hand, too. Stretch and keep your hand still for about 12 seconds and fix your gaze at the outstretched arm. You might want to try other parts of your body too. Just ensure that you pay attention to all you do.

4. **A Three-Minute Study of an Insect**

Insects are almost everywhere. Good places to enjoy this exercise will be in your garden and at a park. Take a walk to a park and sit under a tree. Look closely at the bark of the tree. You would surely see an insect. It might be on the grass or at the branches of a flower/plant. Any one you notice first is good to go with.

Get close to the tree or plant but not too close; make sure you look around closely so as not to disturb other insects. Study the movement of the insect(s). Put close attention to where they started their journey. You might be fortunate enough to see them carry particles (if walking with their friends and neighbors) from one place to another.

Your focus will improve if you could pick one insect out of many and use your sight to monitor it for 3 minutes. This period of mindfulness might look long to you because of their movement, resemblance, body structure, and color.

5.   Colored Bottle Study

All you need for this exercise are different-colored bottles. You can have a mix of plastic and ceramic jars. Place them on a table and create a little distance from it. Stare at them as long you can. Start with three different colors which might be a mix of your favorite. You might tend to focus more on one color than on others; your aim is to be mindful of a specific color. The more you are aware of your choice bottle, the more your focus is strengthened.

Whenever your mind wanders away from your task, try to bring it back as quickly as possible. You may also want to write down those thoughts that flash through your mind during the process of this exercise.

6.   Jazz Music Break Down

The genre of this music might not be your pick but listening to it will help boost your focus level. Notice that there is a soft combination of musical instruments for this kind of music. Your attention should be on the timing of each of the instruments used.

Your first assignment is to get into the rhythm. How does music make you feel? Your present environment is not your concern for now, and that's why it will be best for you to do this exercise behind closed doors. The next thing to do is to channel your emotions to your thought. To do this, bring your feelings to align with your ideas through the music. There is an emotion that follows the piano, while the drum set is different also. Just flow with the music and don't wander away.

7. Smell Exercise

This exercise will work well for those who have a strong sense of smell. But it doesn't leave out every other person. Every time there is a strong smell, try and be a detective. Exert effort to trace where the smell is coming from. It might be the smell of a coffee, perfume, flower, or even food. Let your brain interpret the scent and enjoy the feeling they bring to you. You might go further to know the intensity as in the case of food. You might want to determine whenever the food is boiling or burning.

8. Movie Report

Your kind of movie might be romance or action. Your focus on film should be on how well you can tell another person about the most exciting part. If you can do this successfully, then move a step higher by becoming the movie to talk about to a friend. Doing this will require more serious attention than the movie. You are both the actor and director here. Detailed and specific information will be required on all you do and how you do them. This exercise will allow you to comprehend your actions and will most likely expose the intent behind them.

9. Feel your Pulse

No tool will be required to carry out this exercise. For you to be successful on this one, you first need to monitor how you breathe. Put attention on how you inhale and exhale. At what rate? And under what conditions do you breathe either fast or slow? You might notice that when you are a bit anxious, your breathing changes compared to when you are confident.

Be in a comfortable position, either on the floor or chair. Make sure your body is relaxed. Take a slow, but deep breath and launch into the experience. Focus on the subtle sound of your pulse and breathe. You might also want to experience how slowly your chest expands.

The attention given at first might not be as perfect as a golden plantain. Don't be hard on yourself. Do it repeatedly and enjoy the tranquillity that accompanies the natural thought pattern of this exercise.

10. See with your Eyes Closed

Since the eye is the organ than gives sight, it is the most accessible doorway to most distractions. We don't need to pluck out those eyes to stop seeing them. But we can also rely on it to strengthen our focus.

Go to a public place but with few people around, close your eyes, and focus on your feelings. If you are successful in combining your emotions well, step further in this exercise by going to where there is a crowd. Notice the sounds around you — the footsteps, chant, and chat. Can you still concentrate on your feelings? If yes, then try as much as possible to understand what is going on around you. Once you get to this level, your mindfulness has increased to a definite high.

11. Conscious Listening

This exercise is similar to the movie report, only the group of friends involved is different. Speak to your friends about having a heart-to-heart discussion. It will be interesting if you have a mix of males and females.

Group yourselves into groups of two from opposite sexes and form a listening clique. Ensure there is a coordinator that monitors this exercise. Discuss any subject you all agree to converse with friends only. When your partner is done, switch roles and be the one to listen. Timing will be necessary for this exercise, say five minutes. When the clique is done with their first ten minutes, the coordinator then announces for both of you to share each other's story as you heard it. Ensure that you use the exact word, phrase, and possibly the gesture as you were told. Make your partner's story appear personal to you.

At the end of everyone's session, the coordinator then allows everyone to comment on their experience. At the end of this game, everyone would have been able to achieve some level of strengthened attention.

12. Conscious Eating

Conscious eating here does not mean impulse eating or feeding, influenced by emotions. It entails the awareness needed when eating your daily meals. And since food is essential for our daily nutritional needs, we could both enjoy the feelings attached to it through mindfulness. The satisfaction will come when you have an understanding of why you eat. The thought of the reason should be far from hunger. It's about building a relationship with food.

Let's start with the process of cooking and the smell attached to it. Maybe you have not been conscious enough to absorb the feelings attached to "pre-cooking and pre-eating." Your aim when eating shouldn't be to swallow. What about the coloring, the garnishing, and cutlery arrangement?

Enjoy your next meal by taking it in bits. Bite, steadily chew the food, and allow yourself to experience the feeling of each spoon. While eating, you may ask yourself if the emotion attached to it is right. Don't eat because everyone seems to be eating at that moment. You have likely been doing this before, but you might not enjoy this exercise if that is what motivates you to eat. Remember that our aim for this exercise is to be able to concentrate on every detail of what you eat.

13. Conscious sitting and standing

We often do this without taking into account how frequently we do this. It will best describe acute mindfulness if you account for your daily activities. Sitting and standing is one that could boost laser focus ability. One is likely to rise and rest many times in a day without taking cognizance of it. Your job requirement might force you to do so.

But you could also build mindfulness in doing the same. Be in charge of the decision to either stand or sit. It might not sound easy at first, but it's worth the try, and you may even remember after you have walked a few meters. Once you register this consciousness as a new vocabulary in your mind, you will see yourself getting familiar with it.

14. Word Count Exercise

Try this exercise with your favorite book, magazine or newspaper. Start with five paragraphs and read them. After you must have absorbed the content, begin the word count. Count each word from the first paragraph to the last and repeat the process in descending order. It will be essential for you to note each word you count. Keep to memory the usage, function, and intent. The more you do the counting, the more you are aware of the words.

You could also commit to mind the number of words in each paragraph. When you are sure of your achievement for five sections, you can proceed to 10, 20, or even a whole chapter.

The Crucial Link Between your Brain and your Belly

One crucial factor to consider when thinking of a healthy lifestyle is the food you take. The traditional benefits of food spans from medicinal to nutritional; it is the most considered build-up to all-around soundness of the body. As it is said, "You are what you eat."

Individual meals are prescribed to patients based on their illness, imperfections, and symptoms. And this has proven to be effective over time. Asides genetic factors, feeding has the capability to change the growth level of individuals. An example will be a comparison between well-fed children to malnourished ones.

There is a connection between our productivity level and the food we eat. You would agree that not eating adequately has a way of telling on the brain. Remember when you were famished; it was as if nothing is working in you. The only thought that filled your mind is the consumption of food. This feeling is not strange because the presence or absence of food has been proven to regulate your activeness, alertness, energy, and willingness. When you're hungry, your ability to focus was reduced, and your mood was not at its best.

Your brain suffers when you are hungry because it can't perform to its highest potential. You won't be able to focus on a task; and even when you do, it is most likely not to be excellent because your blood sugar level is not regulated.

1. **Almonds**

This fruit contains fiber and protein, which are known to increase feelings of fullness. Eating this nut allows you to consume fewer calories per day. It also has an antioxidant called phytic acid which protects against oxidative stress. Ensure you consume the brown layer of the skin

2. Salmon

The presence of high omega-3 fatty acids content is what makes salmon able to boost memory and mental performance. You might not get disappointed quickly. A fish oil supplement can also achieve optimum results for depression.

3. Green Tea

This natural tea contains L-Theanine. This property is a component that increases calmness and tranquillity. It works perfectly with another part called caffeine by making it release steadily. Caffeine boosts focus and alertness. You could stay active all day when you enjoy it in its powdery form.

4. Bananas

Banana contains glucose which releases energy to the body. Eating a banana a day will complement the daily need for glucose. It is also great as a between-meals food as it will fill you up. You may try it with a peanut for a composed snack and experience the refreshing moment all day. The presence of pectin in banana regulates blood sugar level and reduces appetite by reducing the vastness of the stomach

5. Eggs

An egg contains an abundance of Omega-3 fat and a B-vitamin called choline, among other nutrients. It works to enhance the mental reactive sensors and also raises the High-density lipoprotein which is connected to reduce the possibilities of many diseases

The nutrient in egg appears more as one of its calories is higher than most foods. These nutrients can help to keep the hunger away for an extended period.

6. Brown Rice

The magnesium present in brown rice relieves stress and boosts productivity. Unlike white rice, the energy present is released slowly to increasingly build-up power throughout the day. The health benefit is contained in its whole grain form. Another fantastic component is the low glycemic index. The glycemic index shows how fast a food raises a person's blood sugar. Brown rice is rated as an average GI food making it easy to consume.

7. Dark Chocolate

Once the concentration of cocoa is 70 percent or higher in chocolate, then the nutritional value is a thing to celebrate. The flavonoids found in chocolate as well as in other fruits and vegetables has an anti-allergic, anti-inflammatory, and anti-tumor properties. Flavonols also reduce the risk of heart disease, cancer, and stoke. It seeks to lower blood pressure and helps in blood flow, leaving your body active all day. Once your heart is perfect, your brain wouldn't have any issues functioning.

8. Blueberries

Blueberries are noted for its antioxidant properties that fight disease, as well as able to stop belly bloat. The hidden benefit of this fruit is that it enhances cognitive ability. Your brain is set for the day with this fruit.

5 Ways to Develop Unwavering Self-Discipline

Learning does not stop at the moment of doing; it continues until the behavior is personalized. You wouldn't approve of a child's knowledge until it becomes part of the child's way of life. For example, after a child has learned cleanliness in school but still litters his room with toys, you would agree that he has not applied the knowledge to his daily life. The assertion might not be accurate if he keeps a clean room in the first week of learning but fails to continue after the following weeks. It is not because of failed memory; it is due to a lack of desire, drive, and motivation to persist. We can generally say that he is not disciplined enough to continue.

Self-discipline entails every effort to control yourself. This definition might sound vague as you feel that you have always been in charge of your decisions. It might be correct, but what about your impulses, emotions, and feelings? Those are the big cards of your successes and failures, depending on how well you have mastered the game. The ability to consciously commit yourself to fulfill your goals irrespective of varying feelings can be termed self-discipline.

By now, you must have improved your level of focus. Sustaining this achievement is why self-discipline is necessary as this will form another habit in you. The process will not be a fast one but will surely help your productivity level and sustain any of your learned positive behavior.

It will begin with a steady approach to carefully analyze what you do in line with becoming better. For example, trying the conscious listening exercise will allow you to adapt to the changing conditions of different sounds in your environment, and allows you to flow with the circumstance without affecting your mindfulness (inner self).

An acute understanding of this subject will help you to achieve an excellent result to maintain a top-notch focus, beat laziness, and defeat procrastination. Take to heart the following nuggets to sustained self-discipline:

1.   Identify and Analyze your Triggers
Positioning yourself in a safe zone is not only necessary when involved in a hazardous task; it should be natural. Our helmet here is to sustain self-discipline is to identify the triggers that cause distraction. This action is not only aimed at achieving success alone but digging deep to the root to measure the cause of its repeated failure. What causes you to lose focus? What are those factors that push you to perform the task in the future?

Do a proper assessment of those elements and be sincere as much as possible. The same thing goes to those triggers that increase your productivity level. It is possible to have the same factor contributing to both increased productivity and procrastination. For example, your partner at your workplace might inspire you to do more through his unrelenting attitude to work, and at the same time, make you an addict to the digital world.

Once you are clear on your triggers, propose alternative options to scale through. Try to write them down. It may involve the same way you write your to-do-list. Create another not-to-do-list to counter those issues. Through this approach, you won't see yourself falling into the same pit time and again.

2. Be Sure of Your Purpose

A strong desire to win will be required to maintain an unwavering self-discipline course. Ask a series of questions. Why do I want to read a chapter of a book a day? Why must I eat cereal once in every two days? Self-awareness is necessary to keep you going. Analyze your feelings and emotions to be sure that you are not playing on them. Have a clarity that your pre-learned behavior is not on a temporary assumption or influenced by the rhythm of the moment.

3. Build a Motivation Block

Create a system that will continuously fuel your passion to commitment. It might be a competitive environment where you can outwork or outperform others. Since you can measure your progress with hardworking colleagues, your progress will be on track.

Another motivation block can be to introduce a reward-and-punishment tool. The reward tool might be to buy an item for yourself every time you achieve or surpass a target. It might also be to take a time-out to have fun. You might think of paying a friend an agreed sum of money as your punishment tool. Just ensure that your motivation is keeping you going.

4.   Choose a Model

Look to the outside world to keep on track. Search for someone who has been on the path you want to tread. He/she should be someone who has mastered the habit and have proven to develop over time. He might be your college professor, your gym instructor, or your spiritual head. Be sure you are right on whom to choose. Get ready to follow whatever you are told to do. It might look rigorous at first, but the desired outcome will surface.

5.   Design a Strategy

Here is one of the essential tools to maintain self-discipline: Develop a plan to work with. Discipline is not automatic as it involves a process of building. Your action must comprise of a deadline and an achievable step-to-step guide. The good thing about these mini milestones is that you will be able to measure your progress. And a sound reward system can keep you focused and master an active control system.

The aim of this plan is not to get overwhelmed by your goals. Progress is the primary fuel that will push you farther to actualize your strategies. Deadlines also will force you to gather all resources at your reach to achieve success on a specific date.

Chapter Five: Goal Setting For Success

You may have spent a lot of time wondering why things don't just seem to work out well for you. One time you have a dream burning in your mind with full plans to accomplish that dream, and the next thing you know, it is gone, and you have accomplished nothing. You may have also spent a lot of time in thoughts, comparing yourself with people who achieve things with ease; people who it seems were simply born to be successful. These people know what they want, state what they want, and follow it with all their zeal until they see it achieved.

There is little or no secret attached to these people and their success. The only thing that differentiates you from them is the ability to set goals. These people don't only work hard; they work smart. And working smart entails setting strong and workable goals. Without goals, life would simply be directionless, and a directionless life will be an unproductive life with nothing to live for.

Most of the time, only a few of us sit down and chart a course for our lives. Take life like a stormy sea, with you and your boat floating on that sea. There is every possibility of you being taken off course. But if you have a compass, it will be easier for you to find your way home after the storm has subsided. Your goal is like a compass that helps to put you back in check after a period of going astray.

In this chapter, we will be going through some of the basics of setting goals. What are the best techniques and tips that you should employ while setting goals? How realistic and workable should your goals be so that they don't end up frustrating you as you work towards achieving them?

Concepts Associated with Goal Setting

Before we begin to explore the necessary techniques for goal setting, there are some concepts about goal setting that you have to understand. If these are not well-understood, then I tell you that the whole process will end up filled with failure. The most important question of all is:

Why do I need to set goals? This is a very personal question, and you would need to provide a personal answer before you can go on. Without providing an answer, you will never be able to connect with the goal-setting activity on a more personal level.

In setting goals, these two things will help you out in forging something that works.

- **What are your goals?** What exactly is it that you want? Do you want to land on the moon someday? Do you need to lose more than 100 pounds with 6 months? Are you planning to win an Oscar before you turn 40? Identify these goals because they will provide you with instant clarity. The goals will help your mind as a compass to accomplishment. In fact, an identified goal sets your heart on fire like no other.
- **Why do you want to accomplish these goals?** I can't tell you anything more important in goal setting. Without a purpose or a reason, your goals are as good as nuts. Take some time off and evaluate your reason for setting these goals? Do you need to get a good car so it would help you feel good around your peers or because it will help you move faster around town? Are you trying to lose weight because someone insulted you about your plus-size or because you simply want to live healthier? As you may know, a goal set for a selfish reason never gets to see the light of day as regards its achievement. With a

concrete and well-laid purpose, your goal setting will be a whole lot more easily.

Forms of Goals

To effectively set a goal, you need to understand what kind of goal you are setting. There are different types and finding the right one will help you a long way. The most important form of goal categorization is the one that is done based on the timeline. These include:

1. **Short-Term Goals:** These goals are those that can be achieved in a short time, say within a period of six months or less than a year. When setting such goals, you should look at those that can be easily achieved so that you can go forward with the next goal.
2. **Long-Term Goals:** These goals take a longer space of time before they fully actualized. They even take years. Some of these goals make include learning and starting up a business, raising a child, or beating cancer.
3. **Lifelong Goals:** Goals like these may take you a lifetime to accomplish. The thing with lifelong goals is that you may never know when they will be accomplished. At some point, you are bound to get frustrated and want to give up. But you should note that lifelong goals as built on the achievement of long-term and short-term goals. A goal example of a lifelong goal is a child with a dream of becoming the President.

10 Goal-Setting Techniques to Achieve your Goals Faster

1. **Identify the Benefits of Achieving that Goal.**

It is one thing for you to know the purpose of following a goal through to the end, and it is a different thing to understand the benefit of achieving that goal. If a goal comes with no benefit, either for you or the people around you, then there will be no need to pursue it because even your mind will feel frustrated trying to compel you to action. Knowing what is in it for you will be enough drive to help you sit up and get to work. For an exercise, pick your goal-setting book and jot down some of the benefits that you will enjoy if a goal is achieved. Think long and hard while filling those spaces with answers.

2. Set Compatible Goals.

When trying to set goals you can easily achieve, it is necessary that you make them compatible with each other. Setting incompatible goals make you waste your time and energy. Soon you will find yourself feeling very stressed out and weak, unable to go on with the pursuit of your goals. One goal may be to spend more time with people and make new friends, and another goal may be to learn how to be on your own more often and focus on a given task. These two are conflicting. You can't spend more time with friends and still have enough time to complete the task. When putting down goals, it is necessary that you look into each of them and measure their compatibility with the rest of them on the list.

3. Create a Standing Balance.

Don't allow yourself to get too involved in trying to achieve a particular goal that you begin to ignore the others. Life works with balance. You should learn to share your time equally amongst all of your goals. It will make no sense that you succeed in one aspect and fail in the other. You might be experiencing a lot of success in one aspect of your life, but when you discover that the other aspect is unfinished, it might be too late.

4. Ask for Help When Necessary.

That is why they are called goals; you can't achieve them alone. There are a lot of people around you who will be willing to help you out with your goals if only you will agree to be humble and meet them. For every goal you may want to achieve, there is someone out there who has achieved that goal a long time ago. You should connect with them and find out how they did it, what obstacles they faced, and how they overcame.

When analyzing your goals, try to identify places in which you can be helped so that you will be more specific in seeking that help. These can include skills you make need to acquire or knowledge to be gotten.

5. Focus on the Things that will Enhance your Goals.

When making your schedule for the day, try to basically consider those things that will add value to your goals. Those are the things that you should consider the most. They should take up more of your time. There are other activities that you can modify to help you create more time for these other activities. Do not hesitate to do those.

6. There is Work to be Done, and No One will Help you Do it.

This is probably the most important thing you should know about goal setting. It is not just about writing down the goals in a book and staring at them all day long. There is a lot more attached to it, and most of it is work. You should learn to take up the responsibility that will be associated with the work that you are about to do. At some points, if you begin to experience failure, your mind will be eager to help you shift blame. Please overcome this pleasurable temptation. It will lead you nowhere tangible. Instead of allowing yourself to get trapped in the web of complaints and excuses, make up your mind that no matter what happens, that goal must be accomplished.

7. Do Away with Potential Interruptions and Distractions

You will encounter a lot of distractions and interruptions on your way to achieving your goals. They will come in many disguises, and parade themselves as things that need to be accomplished urgently. Perhaps some of them might be legit, so you would need you the discretion to be able to select the wheat from the tares. Most of them will simply be time wasters on a mission to kill your time and slow you down. The ability to successfully differentiate which activities are worth your time is a very important skill you will need to master if you must accomplish those goals.

8. Stay Open to Change

A lot of unexpected things can arise, and you may need to make some changes to your goals. It may be a positive change, but a change all the same. Once you notice that something unplanned and unforeseen is about to take place, that will be the perfect time to make evaluations and know those things that can be changed. You can also keep your mind open and look for opportunities in them.

9. You Will Need a Level of Persistence

Working towards your goal is not all you may need to do to get them to achieve. Putting in all the required effort at the initial stage and then faltering at the end will only make you regret the whole process. Persistence is the necessary spice that makes your hard work pay off. You will surely meet a lot of hard bumps on your way but keeping up with everything required of you is something that will guarantee you success in the long run. Remember that all the things you will be doing now will only be short-term sacrifices, and they will provide you with long-term pleasures. It is up to you.

10. Constantly Review your Goals

Reviewing your goal will help you to identify any progress you may have made over time. It also provides you with the opportunity to pinpoint the places where you may have failed. When reviewing your goals, ask yourself questions about how far you have come achieving the goal, what steps should be changed towards achieving the goal with more speed and if you are still on the right track. Goal review will also help you motivate you towards performing better.

7 Things you Need to Know About Setting the Right Goals

I always tell my audience to find the right goals to set. There are goals for you, and then there are goals that you shouldn't bother setting because they will yield no value to your life. If the right goals are not being set, then there is every possibility of you losing focus even before they are accomplished. Setting the right goals will take some time. The right goals don't just come to you prepared. You might need to brainstorm some ideas before you find which goals are right for you and which aren't. But there are some general techniques you can put in place to help you with your selection. Here are some of them:

1. **The Right Goal can be Measured**

Your goals should be goals that can be easily measured to find out how successful you have been with them. If you write down your goals and break them into bits, then there should be an avenue for you to be able to tick them and measure success. A goal that can be measured should be one that is specific, like, "I will lose ten pounds before the months runs out." or "I should finish writing my next book before the year runs out." All of these are examples of measurable goals. These kinds of goals make it easy for you to track success.

2. **The Right Goals can be Managed**

If you find yourself constantly being overwhelmed by a goal, it may mean that it is not the right goal for you. The right goal is that goal that you can break down into smaller goals. These smaller goals will serve as milestones that will build up to the accomplishment of the main goal. Breaking your goals into smaller bits will help you keep track of its success rate.

3. The Right Goal can be Achieved No Matter the Hurdles that Come with it

Each goal on your goal list must have a point with which you can finally measure success. If your goal does have that point where you can look back and say you have come a long way, then it is an abstract goal. Setting a goal and saying, "I want to sell my products" is not a goal. How many of those products do you want to sell? If you don't clearly define what an achievement is for you, then you won't be able to reward yourself even when you sell a thousand of those products. In your mind, the goal remains unachieved, and soon, you will give up on it. The main thing is to place a target on all your goals.

4. Any Obstacles Against the Accomplishment of the Right Goals can Easily be Detected a Long Way Off

If you run into unforeseen problems while trying to execute a goal, you can take that as a point that the goal wasn't meant for you all along. The right goal is one that allows you to detect any future problems while you are making a review of the steps required to accomplish it. Once these problems present themselves in the initial stage, all you have to do is put in measures to mitigate their effect.

5. The Right Goal will have a realistic and workable deadline

Every goal needs a timeframe, a period with which it should be accomplished. With a set deadline, your mind is moved to work to produce a result. Once you have come up with a timeframe within which your job should be accomplished, you will find out that a sense of urgency will be instantly attached to the job. And having a sense of urgency is something I mentioned earlier, which will help you with your goal-setting venture. There should be enough time that will help you reach the goal, yet the time shouldn't be too long to get you uninterested in the goal. But you should put the magnitude of your goal into consideration when setting a timeframe, so you don't end up deceiving yourself.

6. **The Right Goal can be Easily Visualized**

If you don't have a picture, then you don't have a destination. Does our goal give you a picture? If it does, how tangible and real, is it? When making a review of your goals, picture yourself accomplishing the goal. Picture yourself holding your complete novel in your hands. Picture yourself with your degree in three years' time. Picture yourself in your car. The stronger and clearer the picture, the easier it will be to get the motivation to work towards it. You can easily rejuvenate a dull and unmotivated day by imagining the results of your success. Your goals must have a picture.

7. **The Right Goal will Always Have a Long-Term Value for your Life**

Finally, the right goal is a goal that has rewards that will stay with you for a lifetime. Although there are the right goals with short-lived rewards, most of the right goals always come with rewards that stay longer. When setting each goal, try to analyze and identify the benefits associated with each of them. They may include financial freedom, mental rest, physical health, and psychological stability. Whatever they may be, just know that identifying them will help you a long way.

The Best Ways to Reward Yourself for Completed Goals

First, you have to understand that no one will reward you more than you can reward yourself. You deserve to be rewarded, especially when you have successfully completed a task, herculean or not. Reward your body. Reward your mind. Reward your soul. Reward yourself no matter how little it may be. It definitely goes a long way. To reward yourself is to tell your mind and brain that it has done a good job and will encourage it to do more. Once you can establish this in your mind, you will find out that it will be a lot easier for you to work because your body will be looking forward to that reward received after the first completed job.

To start the process of rewarding yourself, you have to know what the reward will be for. Take out a pen and book and jot down whatever you may want to reward yourself for. Make sure that you have a detailed and comprehensive list before going ahead with the rewarding process. If not, you will only be deceiving yourself. There are many ways for you to reward yourself, and I will introduce you to some of them. But you should also note that your rewards should not come in such a way that they will negate everything you have just worked for. That will be the wrong reward system. The most important things to consider when selecting reward are:

1.   It Should Have Long-Lasting Value
The reward should be of value to you in any way possible. Don't just go for a reward that will provide you with instant happiness; go for something more concrete and deep. Look for a reward that will gratify even your soul. You can go for a spiritual experience and see life in a whole new way.

The core of your selection should be of self-compassion. Be kind to yourself, because of the benefits of self-kindness are numerous and overwhelming. It should not be a one-time reward but should be practiced as much as possible whenever a task is completed.

2.   It Infuses Positivity

Your rewards should also drive you towards accomplishing more than you have achieved before. Acknowledge of all of the things that you have achieved now but strive to do more in no time. Your reward should remind you about the importance of not being too hard on yourself.

3.   There Should be a Necessary Balance in the Reward System

Don't allow your reward system to go over the top. There has to be a sensible balance. The reward should not exceed the size of the completed tasks that necessitated them.

4.   Tone it Down

Sometimes your reward can come from within you, just something inside of you. It can just be a quiet day or moment when you sit and reflect everything on your journey. That can be a clear moment of enlightenment that will assist you in your future journey.

5.   **You don't have to spend a lot to reward yourself.**

Rewards can simply be the things you enjoy doing.

6.   **It should be easy to achieve as fast as possible.**

Here are some quick ways in which you can reward yourself after completing a task. There is a wide variety, and it is up to you to choose the one that suits you.

Beat Procrastination

1. Go to a concert.
2. Visit a carnival or a music festival.
3. Go see a movie with some friends.
4. Listen to a captivation podcast.
5. Plan a night out with family members.
6. Enjoy a magazine read with a glass of cold juice.
7. Soak your body in a hot bath in the bathtub.
8. Stream some danceable music online.
9. Stream some interesting documentaries on Netflix.
10. Go for a long walk in your favorite park.
11. Join an exercise or dance class.
12. Visit an art gallery and see inspiring artwork.
13. Treat yourself to a foreign meal.
14. Visit a spa and get a royal treatment.
15. Have a picnic at a nearby beach.
16. Attend a sports event and cheer your favorite team.
17. Have a small get-together and celebrate with your friends.
18. Engage your hands in an art form that you love or in gardening.
19. Reorganize your room and closet.
20. Take photos of yourself.
21. Get a new hairdo.
22. Have a free day where you lie around, doing what you want or doing nothing at all. (But don't allow the pleasure of such a day get into your head. Once the day is over you go back to your routine.)
23. Write a short story about yourself and share it on social media.
24. Buy a new perfume with a fragrance that you love.
25. Get yourself some new clothes and discard off some old ones. Or you can give them out too.
26. Travel to a place you have always wanted to travel to.

Chapter Six: New You, New Routines

Growth in itself is the influence of greatness and achievement. Life has taught us to improve on everything, even the most common of things. Human beings are not separate from becoming better. We have come to learn the hard way through trial and error. And for this, history has related the importance of self-growth and the attitude needed to attain this level of excellence.

From the values required to the skills and knowledge needed, all these virtues can be learned. And the truth lies in the opportunity life has presented to learn continuously. The more we see the need to adopt new techniques and learn skills, the more comfortable living becomes. And since we don't live in isolation, the people around us get motivated through our process of learning. For example, renowned leaders invest a great time in knowledge and research; for that's one of the ways to break through to attainment.

Learning comes with many hurdles to climb, and no one says it's easy to adopt a new behavior. The fuel to sustain this change mostly comes from proven structures. One of them has to do with you. It is a positive attitude to see beyond your immediate mindset and embrace the newness you have seen people become. Once your mind is open, every other thing that relates to tranquility, togetherness, goal setting, and discipline will be natural to you. Your mind will now become fertile ground for breeding positive habits. You would be able to think brightly and expect the best to happen always.

A new routine begins with a firm conviction to do things differently. You might be tired of the results you make per time, and you feel something is missing. You are correct! If you have been thinking in this direction, then, you are ready to make an impact. This level is the foundation of your success. It is now evident that you are prepared to stand out without losing your uniqueness.

Don't be overwhelmed with the desire to get great results; it is attainable. But you need to understand that it is not automatic. The process involved needs you to review your choices creatively. You might also need to break down your preferences, emotions, and thought patterns to sooth the new routine you have chosen. Be sure that trends do not influence your choice to do things differently. Trends are like fashion; they come and vanish with time.

8 Ways to Create Great Habits that Lead to Success

The undeniable truth about success is that it has to be maintained. Sustaining excellence, achievement, and productivity starts with the most ignored principle. This standard is what I call the "principle of continuous growth." It deals with a conscious effort to regularly checkmate human composition to become better. Checkmating here means consistent appraisal of our emotions, skills, abilities, values, and attitudes to fit into the intended learning process. You need to ask questions to look for solutions instead of dwelling on the adverse reports.

How humans spend time goes a long way in accounting for productivity. The attitude put to the time also has a significant effect on whether the moment is valid or not. Certain elements might have acclimatized themselves to our views, making us prone to its negative impact. Such properties become our daily reference, disposition, belief, assumption, perception, and doctrine. Those are what result in habit, and we unconsciously repeat the pattern in our daily lives. The excellent news about a habit is that it can be learned. Your awareness of this routine and willingness to change is what matters most. I will outline below some great patterns that will inspire you to a successful life.

1. **Identify the Kind of Routine you Want.**

When a destination is known, the path to get there will be quite straightforward. See to it that you have convinced yourself of the kind of habit you want to break. This realization should be what matters most to you at the moment; a top priority that should not be postponed. Engage this decision in your thoughts consistently, but don't get carried away.

Identifying a negative habit is great; positioning your mind to replace it with a positive one will be more fulfilling. Satisfy your conscience and willpower to get set on the new journey of an improved person. It is necessary to be inwardly persuaded because that is the fuel that keeps the consistency going.

This stage of identification needs a proper breakdown of your engagement. Let's start with the little things that keep you busy like gossip. You need to know when and how the chat starts if your new routine is to get focused on writing a 1000-word report on safety per day every time you close from work. Then shut down any signal that suggests a delay in time and mental capabilities. While it might have been a frequent occurrence to chat at the parking lot, decide to shorten the discussion when you notice it's going south. You are in charge here, and that's the reason you need to be sincere. This is just an example, and yours might be different.

Also, realize that you will be in charge of your activities since you could predict what you desire. No one forced you into it; it's a personal choice so that mindfulness will set in. You would be able to position yourself to the present target and not get overwhelmed with the uncertainties of the future.

With the awareness of the present, you will be able to channel your energy and resources to achieving a present task. It will be more comfortable to accept the feelings and thoughts pattern that follows awareness.

Knowing what you want to achieve now and in the future places you on what it takes to attain them. Sacrifice is top of them. The newly identified routine is most likely not to follow your conventional way of life. And if yours is completely different, then get ready to adapt to the changes. Your time on the social network might need to change and hangout moments will adjust. Whatever it is you feel will be affected, prepare for it so as not to cause a delay along the path of successful attainment.

2. Start From your Current Position.

It might sound ridiculous when you see yourself not going at a fast pace. But the truth is, that is the perfect pace for you. Remember that habit constitutes a whole part of us, and the significant change won't come as quick as you imagine. The will to move is the necessary speed you need here.

Think of it as like building your muscles. You should know that the physical build-up won't surface in a day. You might be longing to stick to reading for three hours every evening. Understand that you would have used most of your productive moments during the day, and the possibility of reading at a stretch is slim since you are starting new. Why not start with thirty minutes and master the art for the first two weeks. Once you are consistent with the half an hour routine, increase the duration progressively. Ensure that you have established the behavior, and then seek to maintain it.

3. Recreate your Surroundings.

You are not the perfect composition of yourself without your environment. Some triggers stabilize your old habit, and most of them are within your reach. First, identify what they are and how they start. Those triggers might not signal delay and procrastination, but in the real sense, they are the villain.

Your new habit might be to start a new diet, but it seems your kitchen is still stuck with your old meals. It will be best to remove those foods or probably don't shop for them. It will be hard to focus on your new routine because the more you see those foods around, the harder it becomes to do away with them.

Reorganize your house, office, table, and even wardrobe to suit your expected behavior. The more you clear off distractions, the better your chance of success. The idea here is to get rid of the energy that makes learning difficult for you and replace it with good ones.

4. Move with People that Encourage you.

Your motivation for sticking to a learned behavior will be boosted when you are accountable to your friends. It is not compulsory to report to your acquaintance. It might be a colleague at work or your mentor. Choose someone you trust enough to criticize your report.

Your focus at this point is that you are not on the path of newness alone; there are external bodies that support your new habit. You will achieve optimum results if you choose someone successful in learning your selected routine. This way, he will be able to guide you constructively.

The significant result you want to see in the new routine can also be fostered when you see it as teamwork. Imagine your clique deciding to start a new habit. Every one of you will be motivated to put in your best. One good thing you will keep in mind is that "there is someone next to me I can always refer to," and he/she will be your most active encouragement. It will be difficult for you to stop. You might decide to speak your friends into learning a new behavior to enhance a fast rate of the result.

5.   Tell Others about your Plan.
Most people are scared of failure, and failure in itself is an ailment that can be avoided. A better way humans prevent it is by pushing their energy to succeed. Think of yourself as someone that can be trusted with information. Confidentiality is not the highlight here but openness and accountability; knowing that a piece of you has been pre-committed to someone else. You will have to stick to your habit as a matter of necessity because you won't want to disappoint them.

You might start by informing some of your followers on social networks, friends, family members, and colleagues. Tell them beforehand and continuously engage them in your commitment routine. You might not want to disappoint them by backing off. Each time you face the temptation of going back, it's most likely to remember those you have pledged to.

6.   Work Out your New Habit in the Line of the Old.

Beat Procrastination

The energy involved in learning a new pattern is quite different from the complacent comfort of the old one. You will agree that the old routine would have gained access-control over you. Your life would have been repositioned to think and work in that direction. Telling you to dump the old habit immediately will be like asking you to change your skin color thrice a week. It is best to adjust your new behavior with the old one. Remember our first point to start small.

Since you have a plan already, make your strategy as flexible as possible. Be careful here as not to fall prey to negative thoughts. Your tendencies to flow with your daily experience will remind you of negativity, replace them with positive affirmations. As much as you commit to the new behavior steadily, you will get to become better and progress to become a different person.

7. Reward Every Stage of Progress.

Take note of your progress and commend every fulfillment of your desired results. No one can encourage you better than yourself. Reward here should not force you to remain on the spot. If you feel that you have not been motivated to do more while applauding yourself, change how you apply it. Create a conditional reward system. Watch the movie after you have finished off the report. Enjoy the evening with your clique whenever your room is perfectly clean. You can go with the flow of your reward after you have achieved your targets.

8. Engage in Mental Exercise

Your brain is not isolated from your new routine. Your cognitive capabilities have a significant role to play after your willpower. Start with your regular exercise, which might be walking around the park or jogging. While doing any of those exercises, think of the new habits you want to create. Allow your brain to process the information into consciousness, but don't get overwhelmed. This state of knowledge allows you to come into the present realities all the time. You will now be able to avoid distractions because your brain has processed your new routine into its system.

Remember that every makeup of your body matters, and your brain shouldn't be left out. You might also consider doing the exercises that sharpen focus given in this book.

9 Morning Routine to Make Every Day a Good Day

Nature has loaded a bountiful pack of benefits to the early hours of the day. And you will agree that creativity and innovation tend to flow freely during this time. Although this varies from the kind of person you are, it still does not negate how productivity can be achieved. This section will provide activities to perform to maximize your morning. Following them promptly will set the tone for an excellent day.

1.   **Make a Journal of your Thoughts and Use it for your Day.**

The refreshing times of the morning are the best moment to write down what comes to your mind. Every one of your activities during the day might defer you the privilege, and that's why you must maximize the opportunity the early hours give.

Note that you might not need to do this brief exercise the conventional way. Be flexible enough to go with the flow of your thoughts. It might only involve ten minutes of your time. The bright side of journaling your opinion is that your brain is connected to a source of mindfulness. You won't need to stress your cognitive capability to remember the

Beat Procrastination

little things that flood your heart. Now you will be conscious of every idea that would boost your daily experience.

If you will need to create an outline of your thoughts, list them out! You may want to replicate writing the results of daily views. This action will make you reference your success story and remind you of your previous wins. You would also be able to repeat the same routine that brings achievement the next time you face a seemingly related challenge.

2.   Fix your Bed

Does it sound a bit stressing? Yes! Because you have not been practicing it. This simple homemaking skill gives you a sense of responsibility for yourself. Your bed has been able to create the first task of the day successfully. Prove to yourself how successful you want this to be. Every time you do this excellently well, you build a sense of fulfillment.

3.   Don't Conclude on Essential Decisions

Instinct might have guided you before now, but reality is not a game of chance; it will surely play out its rule. Leave your thoughts on the paper and get to finalize them later in the day. Most times, the inner will to make a perfect decision might not be strong enough to give an accurate strategy needed in achieving your goals. Be patient enough to research your perceived inspiration. Your search throughout the day will enhance better mental productivity for the subsequent mornings.

4.   Limit your Choices

This early period of the day forces you to make the inevitable choice for your day. Streamline your selection to your set of values. You might be bugged with the color, type of shirt, shoe, and gown to wear.

The accessories to use might even eat up a lot of your thinking time. Create a routine of your basic needs in the morning and make it practicable. For example, wake up, meditate, choose my clothing, bathe, make coffee, organize, and get set for the day. Simplify your daily choices, and don't make it grievous for yourself.

5. Energize your Body

Think of fitness as another tool to maintain a morning routine. You might not need to go jogging down the street. Your room can allow you to sweat out the energy required for the day. Remember the conditional method of reward you read under creating a habit that leads to success? Make it work for you here also.

Do 15 to 30 push-ups, after which you consider reviewing your activities for the day. You may also want to outstretch your arms and legs and then think about the day's task. Going through those exercises would have prepared your body for the job of the day. Your mind now will be at rest, and your happiness level is increased for the rest of the day.

6. Affirmations

Positive thinking, they say, result in a positive result. Create a mind full of positivity as you make affirmations that will reframe your mind. You often see through your mind; making it a necessity to flush out negativity for the day. Remember, it requires self-talk. Take out time to write your affirmations and read it to yourself. You may start with the simple challenge you had the day before and make good out of it. For example, say, "I walked with excellence today." "I achieved and surpassed targets today." "I am not overwhelmed with success or failure. I excel in my entire task."

7. Focus More on your Inner Self

The strength received from meditation can be enough to pull one through the mental challenges of the day. You will achieve this level of calmness when you separate yourself from both external and inward attachment. Create the willingness to break from the outer world for the moment. Breaking here means creating a focus on yourself, especially your willpower.

Note that this simple exercise requires you to clear off every thought and worry. Your anxiety level must be consciously reduced at this period. Look only at yourself, and not even at social networks. Plan to achieve this rare routine from your evening. No early checking of emails, Facebook, and blogs. Just you alone.

Disassociate yourself from your daily routine of dullness and inactiveness for this brief period in the morning. A 15-minute moment of reflection is a good start for you. See the possibility of attaining success for the day. Reflect on the affirmations you have made and see yourself achieving them. You are feeding your soul at this point to have a winning mindset. And that's how best to describe your day for anyone.

8. Try a Cold Shower

You might not be comfortable with this for the first time. But you can try it a few times and make a habit of it intermittently. Think of the advantages it comes with. Your blood flow tends to increase and makes you active for the day. You would be brave to start and doing this releases dopamine into your body. Your body is then left with the feeling of activeness, motivation, and pleasure. The bath will be an excellent icing to design the day.

9. Plan for a Healthy Breakfast

Understand the healthiness of feeding in the morning. It is essential to combine certain nutrients like protein, minerals, and vitamins together to have a great appetite and to fulfill nutritional needs. Although other nutrients are also necessary, healthy fats and proteins help stabilize your emotions. Remember that your mood needs to be right. Take, for example, a fiber-rich toast and topping. The fiber in this food helps slow digestion, enhancing stable blood sugar. Think of other simple but healthy meals for your breakfast.

6 Evening Routines to Ensure Tomorrow is just as Good as Today.

The best day results from a well-planned evening. Opportunities are loaded in the evening when you take up the challenge to be responsive. Understand what you need to do right before going to bed. Those activities will make up your evening routines. I know that your day might have made you weary, but you can readjust your mood and mental activeness. You can make your rest a blissful experience.

1. Reflect on your Day.

What happened at work today? Why was I issued a query letter? Ask many questions as possible. You deserve to know what has taken up your entire day. Use this period to identify the cause of your actions. Why did I react badly to a customer? Why was I angry during the lunch break? Don't stop with asking questions; break your query down to triggers. See what makes you do a particular thing.

Reflection doesn't mean you should use this period to think of your inadequacies alone. You might want to think of your targets that you met or surpassed. Do a proper assessment of your day's activities to know what goals to set for the other days.

2.   Make a List of your Goals.

Look into the future of productivity and plan what you desire to attain. This process must be intentional because you might not have analyzed the challenges of the day. Design another structure to help you achieve more. Give a proper definition to your destination. Ensure that you eliminate rigidity in your approach to take in the future. After you have drafted out your goals, paste it where you could easily see it. It could be on your reading table or at the back of your door. Build an assurance that you are set for the following morning. Plan for your breakfast, your choice of clothes, and your time to wake up. It might take some time to get ready if you are doing it for the first time. Consistency in setting goals for the next day result in becoming an active organizer in the long run. Waking up to this reality helps you set your mind on attaining targets.

You may also want to read your goals to yourself. Just as you recite your affirmations, your attention in doing this is to activate mindfulness. Live in the reality of having your goals in your mind

3.   Take Time to Read.

Engage your mind in learning something new! Doing this will get you ready for the following day. You might not need to do the long hours as you might be tired of the day's work. You might want to use this period to develop ideas you have written down in the morning. Research also on your challenge at work and learn from the experience of professionals.

4.   Read up Affirmations.

Just like how you began your day with words of positivity, you might consider ending your day with it as well. Since you have reflected and analyzed the happenings of the day, use your conclusion to say beautiful things to your consciousness. You may say, "I was not overwhelmed because of failure." "I achieved better than I did today." "I see myself attaining my career goals." "My tomorrow is active and vibrant, and I stay happy with my friends and colleagues." Design your affirmations to suit your value.

5.   Chat with your Family.

Bonding together as a family is an excellent ritual to practice. Take time out to say personal things to your spouse and children. And if you are single or living alone, find a means of communicating with your family. Every part of your discussion here should center on the family needs. Find out what your daughter desires of you. Inform her also of what you require of her to become successful in life. You might not want to do the job of a life coach every night, but ensure you build intimacy with your family. Also, engage your spouse in an intimate discussion. You may seek ideas relating to your work schedules and pattern.

6.   Don't Give in to Idleness.

Setting yourself up for what to do does not mean doing anything, it means doing a specific task. Think of a job that will boost your mental alertness. Reading, meditation, exercise, cooking, etc. may be an excellent task to perform. Avoid the trap of getting caught up in a massive job for the evening. The blue screen should be a thing to avoid at this time.

Since you need to start small, you may also think of fixing your clutter. Arrange the pile of books on the table and clear your wardrobe.

Chapter Seven: No More Obstacles

7 Ways to Conquer Your Fear of Failure

It is natural to fear. It is one of the things that make us human. Fear will always present itself whenever you are about to embark on a brand-new venture. Yet fear, too, can be very dangerous. It can hold you back from accomplishing what you need to accomplish.

Fear can manifest itself in a lot of ways. There is the fear of heights, the fear of rising water, and the fear of spiders, and so on. But as regards being productive, the fear that relates to us the most is the fear of failure.

Failure is absolutely nothing to be afraid of. Even the richest, the most powerful, and the most successful amongst us have once experienced failure at one point in time or another. So, if you ever fail, you should know that you are not alone. You will get through it.

It is just like falling sick. People put in a lot of measures in place so that they don't fall sick. Unfortunately, no matter how much they try, they ultimately fall sick one day. What do you do in that situation? You don't run away from sickness; you fight it. And once it leaves you, your body learns and adapts so that the next time there is an attack from that pathogen, it will know how to react and protect you.

The same goes for your failure. Learn from it. Build your stamina from it. When it first hits you, it will seem like your world is about to crumble to pieces, but I assure you that it will only be for a moment. These tips will help you manage and overcome the fear of failure:

1. **Stand Up to it.**

Life is a battleground. If you are not ready to fight, then get ready to live a miserable life. Nothing will ever be handed over to you on a platter of gold, except if your family has stacks of gold bars somewhere in the World Bank. To see success, to have accomplishments, you should know that you will have to stand up to your fear of failure. The fear of failure is not failure itself, but it is a strong pathway that leads towards failure. The best you can do for yourself is to push yourself out of that pathway into the pathway of success.

2. **Show yourself some Kindness.**

Don't beat yourself down. Don't be too harsh on yourself. Understand that the fear you have for failure is something natural; but it doesn't mean that you are not good enough. Nobody is good enough; we are all striving to be better. So, don't beat yourself up simply because you did not hit the mark the first time. There are still a lot of open opportunities for you to try and be better.

3. **Understand that Failing Once does not Make you a Complete Failure.**

You only become a total failure when you decide to give and stop chasing. The point where you decide to give up becomes the point where your success story ends, so it all depends on you and how well you choose to maximize your strengths. A lot of successful figures that we look up to today once failed, but that didn't make them consider themselves failures. They kept up with the struggle and brought something admirable.

4. **Feed your Mind with Optimism.**

A lot of people experience failure every day, but that doesn't mean that you must be one of them. A thought will present itself and ask you,

"What if you fail?" I want you to challenge that thought by asking, "What if I succeed?" People fail, and people also succeed. It all depends on the group you decide to identify yourself with. If there is ever going to be a successful person in that field, then it could be you.

5. **Free yourself from the Obsession of Perfectionism**

Many people have been tied down because of the need to get it right the first time. You don't have to get it right the first time. Have that at the back of your mind. Nothing good that was ever created was perfect in one go. Accept the fact that you might not hit your target at first, but that does not mean that you will stop trying. The process of trying to perfect something is itself a learning process. As you keep on doing that, you will keep getting better at it until you become as good as you want to be.

6. **Why do you Fear Failure?**

For some people, the fear of failure stems from all the things they have heard about failure. Others just don't want others to see them as a failure. Hence, they begin to nurture fear for it. Whatever the case may be, try to find out the reason why you fear failure and do well to tackle it early. Are you afraid because you do not fully understand the task at hand? Then do well to understand it better. Are you afraid because you have heard scary stories of people who encountered failure? Then begin to put things in place that will help you overcome failure.

7. **Accept failure for what it is**

Failure is not a monster, nor is it a beast. It can only become as large as tormenting as you want it to be at any point in time. You define what your failure becomes for you. Seeing failure as something that will come and go, something that will come and pass, a fleeting moment in our lives, will help you to overcome your fear for it easily.

7 Strategies for Defeating the Monster of Perfectionism

To be perfect is an admirable quality, and a lot of people will die for that quality, to be free of any form of stain or blemish. Seeking to attain perfection will drive you towards producing work of high standards. To strive for perfection is not wrong in any way; in fact, it is quite necessary to produce work that will stand the test of time.

However, the pursuit of perfection can easily become an obsessive behavior if it is not left unchecked. People who pursue this are referred to as perfectionists, and most of the time, their standards are hardly ever met. This can, in turn, lead to a sort of frustration.

These perfectionists are never happy with anything until it meets their insanely high standards. Conversely, perfectionists seem always to want to put off some tasks simply because they are scared that they will never carry out that task well enough. This can somehow become a killer of productivity because such a person will never want to break into any new adventure and see what happens with it.

A piece of advice I always give to people is that they should learn to work with their perfectionism. Don't allow your high standards to hold you back from performing; instead make it work for you to produce a more admirable job. You do that by starting up the task. Drop your fear of imperfection and just start. Complete the task; and after completion, you can go back and add your touch of perfectionism to it.

The life of a perfectionist is quite boring because nothing new is ever explored. That shouldn't be the case with you. That is why you will need to get over your perfectionist mindset but not your high standards. Understand that perfection can never be attained, ever.

Instead, you can keep getting better and better. Here are some strategies you can employ to help you overcome perfectionism:

1. **Learn to Accept When it is Good Enough When you have Put in your Whole Best.**

Like I clearly stated, perfection is a myth. Even when you think you have achieved it, if you look closer, you will see that there are still flaws. You can literally drive yourself crazy. Try to understand when you have done enough in a particular project. Good is never enough, but your best can always suffice. Don't stress your mind. The best thing to do is to get into the flow and allow yourself to be moved ahead with it. You don't have to produce perfect work; all you have to do is produce your best work.

2. **Understand that Perfectionism is a Time Killer**

There are two major problems I have with perfectionists: the first is that they hardly ever start any task for fear of not producing to their standards. The second is that even when they begin a task, they spend a lot of time going through the steps, repeating them, just to produce a perfect job. The amount of time wasted is even enough to get them to ignore the job and get frustrated. No one is saying that you should not take your time. What I am saying is do not kill your time. These are two different concepts, and they mean different things. Take your time and give your the best. Know when to stop and leave the rest. There is only enough you can give to any project.

3. **Understand that you can Hurt People with your Perfectionist Standards.**

As has been pointed out before, never lower your standards, aim for the best quality, but not necessarily perfection. Perfection is unattainable. One thing about striving for perfection and high standards is that you are capable of hurting the people around you with your standards. Not everyone is like you. Not everyone is a perfectionist like you. Some people only want to put in their best into what they do, and that is all. When you continue to drop the weight of your unachievable standards on them, you can crush them and make them hate you. Nothing they will ever do will ever be enough for you, and this alone is capable of hurting your relationship with them. Make sure to get the best from your employees and workers at all times, but don't become a frustrating master that can never be pleased.

4. **Eliminate the Competitive Mindset.**

For a lot of perfectionists, their character stems from being the best at all times. They want no other person ever to be ahead of them, and it frustrates them when their plans don't go as intended. There is a kind of competition known as the healthy competition, and that is the kind of competition that you should strive towards. Subscribe to the competition that brings out the best in you instead of dragging you towards envy.

Another thing you should understand is that you are your own biggest competitor. All you have to do is develop on yesterday, build on the success you have had in the past. And come to think of it, if you were perfect yesterday, what do you want to do today. Life is an adventure, and perfectionism breaks that adventure. It hinders you from discovering treasures. So, stay free and keep your mind on your own self.

5. **Eliminate Perfectionism Triggers in your Life.**

This will involve looking into a lot of things. Sometimes the people in your life may also be some of the factors causing your obsession with perfectionism. Because they are perfectionists themselves, they will do everything in their power to seek the same from you. Don't buy into that. Perfectionism, as I have explained to you, is stressful. It is left for you to carry out an inner analysis and identify all those things that trigger perfectionism in your life. Quench them.

6. **Reevaluate your Standards**

Perfectionism is a result of excessively high standards. You need to check yourself so you don't wreck yourself. It is not normal to expect a 3-year-old to be able to spell five-letter words correctly without missing out on any letters. But a perfectionist doesn't care. They just want it to be done, and they will have no idea that they are hurting that child.

Ask yourself if your standards are unrealistically high. Once you identify the high standards, you can then tone them down so that everybody benefits from it. You can also ask people around you who will be willing to help you identify those standards that you have to work on.

7. **Allow Imperfection Sometimes.**

You don't always have to perfect. We live in an imperfect world, yet we all enjoy the world and don't want to leave. The truth is that you can do with some imperfection in your life. Leave the bedsheets rough and rumpled as you leave the house. Allow the kids to dress themselves up. Just challenge any perfectionist tendencies you may have and see what happens.

7 Ways in Which Positivity can Manifest Success

Positivity, as a trait, does not mean smiling all the time and always carrying a cheerful look. It is way more profound than that. Positivity really has to do with your overall perspective of life. It is all about what you make with whatever life gives you at the moment, either negative or positive. "When life throws lemons at you, you make lemonade" is one quote that adequately captures the essence of positivity.

Research has proven over time that people who are happier, people who have more positivity in their lives, generally end up more successful than those who do not buy into the message of positivity. Positivity has been linked to better performance and productivity in workplaces. The presence of positive emotions always makes the generation of wonderful ideas. Some major benefits of positivity include:

- **Better mental performance and sharper response to stimuli**. Positive people generally tend to have brains that perform better and produce better results. Their mind travels wider during a brainstorm session, and they can come up with a wide range of ideas for a project. Ultimately, this leads to being more creative and productive people.
- **People tend to get closer to those who already carry a lot of positivity in them.** Positivity in a relationship also helps to build a strong and lasting connection between the parties involved.
- **The health benefits associated with positivity are enormous.** In fact, positivity can cause a person to eat healthier because their minds are always sharp to point out the things they should not be taking into their system. Depression, which is a by-product of negative thinking, has been connected to overweight and junk feeding. A positive mindset will mean a lower heart rate, lower blood pressure, and lower stress. People who stay positive are also known to sleep better.

- **Positivity helps to build a psychology of confidence, boosted self-esteem, and bodily energy.** With such energy to expend, positive people achieve their goals quite faster than non-positive people.

With all of these benefits listed, you can now see that it is quite important that you develop a positive mindset that will fuel your success. The question now is how you can do that. These strategies will help you:

1. **Keep your Focus on all the Good Things in your Life.**

Nobody has it all beautiful for them. We all have our ups and downs, where we face a lot of challenges daily. But the question remains how do you allow those challenges to define you? Of course, you will face the door, but you will also face up. How well do you keep your gaze on the good things in your life? Remember that every single day comes with its own benefits, no matter how bad that day goes. Learn to focus on these benefits for as long as you can.

2. **Learn all the Lessons that Life Throws at you.**

As I have stated numerous times in this book, every failure you come across in your life is a lesson if only you will choose to learn from it. Failures are prone to breed negative thoughts in your mind. These include: "I am not good enough." "I will never be worth it." and "I won't make it." But remember that each time you stumble in the dark, your body learns of obstacles on that path and never makes the same mistake again. That is why you can walk into your room even with the light off and make your way to the switch without hitting your toes on the cabinet.

3.   Encourage Yourself.
No one can talk to you like you can talk to yourself. There is no better motivation than the one you give yourself. Wake up each morning, look at yourself in the mirror, and release transformative mantras into your day. There is something about the words we speak. They possess a very strong creative power that can go ahead and provide us with the best results. Some people use this power to produce very negative results for themselves because they are always talking about the bad in their lives. These thoughts have a way of building strongholds in your mind and control you. Never allow them to do that. Always be the one in control and dictate what comes into your life.

4.   Keep your Mind on the Things Happening in your Present.
The present is your now, your reality at this moment, the things that are currently happening in your life. Some people live their lives for the future, while others live in the past. But I tell you that the most important time to live for is now. Don't lose your existence while chasing other realities.

5.   Keep Positive People and Positivity Around you.
A wall of negative thoughts is always on the rise in our mind, and it totally depends on you to determine if it continues to rise or it crumbles to the ground. You can destroy any form of negative walls by surrounding yourself with positive people and positive things. All of these will assist you in choking down any negativity bridling up around you. Find most people and place them around your life. Talk to them as much as you can and try to learn from them. They have a way of affecting yours into positivity.

6. **Focus on your Goals.**

Negative thoughts are a form of distraction that results because people aren't obsessed with reaching their goals. A mind that stays focused on achieving goals and being the best will never have time to nurture any form of negativity. Keep yourself productive at all times, and continue to focus on how you can achieve more and outdo yourself.

7. **Practice Gratefulness.**

This is one of the greatest tools you can use to activate a positive mindset for success. When you continue to stay grateful and thankful for the things around you, you rarely have time to think about the negatives.

5 Empowering Mantras to Destroy Self-Sabotage and Start Getting Stuff Done.

Funny enough, there has always been this kind of mythological attachments to the word "mantra." It has suffered almost the same fate as "meditation," where someone thinks it can only apply to a Buddhist monk in Tibet or a witch sitting on the Himalayas. Most times, we don't even understand how powerful mantras are and how they can help us generally.

What exactly is a mantra if you should use it? Take it this way: a mantra is a mind tool or a word, sentence, or sound that is used to keep your mind in place and prevent it from wandering off into distraction. Mantras can help you out in different facets of our life if they are employed in the right way. They can help you become more productive. They can help you to stay focused. They can help you to reframe your mind and the thoughts that swirl in it. The possibilities are endless, and that is why it is necessary that you begin to employ mantras in these different facets of your life so that you have the best of it. Here are some mantras that can help you overcome yourself and start getting stuff done.

1. **I accept peace into my life and my daily activities.**

You can assist this mantra to come to fulfillment by visualizing that peace that you desire over and over until it manifests itself. You can make use of this mantra to call peace into any aspect of your life: your mind, your soul, your work etc. When these words are repeated over time, your mind begins to believe them and align towards having them accomplished.

2. **I will strive for the best instead of striving for perfection.**

We have gone through this, and I have explained how toxic perfectionism can be to you and the people around you. Make use of this mantra to overcome a mindset of perfectionism. Before you start an important task, you can repeat it over and over until your mind assimilates it. When you find yourself gradually falling into that mindset of perfectionism, repeat it, and give yourself the required focus.

3. **My mistakes are for my benefits.**

Playing the blame game is always easy, and this mantra is here to help you do the exact opposite of that. Use this mantra when you have made a stupid mistake and feel like you are a failure. Keep it from time to time, even as your mind may try to make you feel bad about the decisions you may have made in the past.

4. **I will focus on my present.**

The mantra is most importantly used when you noticed your mind gradually slipping back to your past or worrying about the future. Remind yourself using this mantra to keep your focus on the present.

5.   **I will meet my deadlines and achieve all my goals**.

Use this mantra at the beginning of each day, first thing after you wake in the morning or while washing your mouth. As you repeat this mantra to yourself, continue to visualize what you accomplished goals will look like. Ruminate over all the exciting benefits open to you as you hit your daily targets.

Conclusion

I want to appreciate you for following me on this journey, for preserving and being here until this moment. In fact, thank you for not procrastinating the reading of this book. I believe you have skipped pages but read through the book with all diligence.

Throughout this book, I have done everything possible to help you understand the concept of procrastination and how it works. We have explored some of the major triggers of procrastination and also the main ways in which you can get over and conquer these triggers. But I can tell you that regardless of the wealth of knowledge hidden in this book, this is not all it takes.

I can tell you that we all face our own different procrastination triggers that are specific to each and every one of us. While reading a book, I am quite certain that you encounter the one that most related to your situation. These are the issues that you need to address as soon as possible. You cannot change everything at once. Try and employ some strategy to your action plan in defeating procrastination.

It is one thing to own the rod, and it is another thing to strike the snake. Most people will go to any length to acquire the rod but will never take action to strike the snake until it bites. I want to tell you that you can break free from the grip of procrastination today, if only you will decide to take action and follow the instructions listed in this book. There will be a point where you will feel like you have failed when it will seem like you should just give up and stop trying, but don't allow that stop you. Promise yourself that you will fight right till the end. Only keep your focus on making some small necessary changes and see your life improve every day.

www.ingramcontent.com/pod-product-compliance
Lightning Source LLC
Chambersburg PA
CBHW031106080526
44587CB00011B/847